SEEING THE INVISIBLE

Mary Irwin

1081

BROADMAN PRESS
Nashville, Tennessee

Dedication

To Jim, my "Schnook" of twenty-eight years

© Copyright 1987 ● Broadman Press
All rights reserved
4250-57
ISBN: 0-8054-5057-2

Dewey Decimal Classification: 248
Subject Heading: SPIRITUAL LIFE
Library of Congress Catalog Card Number: 87-19877
Printed in the United States of America

Library of Congress Cataloging-in-Publication Data

Irwin, Mary, 1938-
  Seeing the invisible / Mary Irwin.
    p. cm.
  ISBN: 0-8054-5057-2
  1. Meditations.   I. Title.
BV4832.2.I795 1987
242—dc19   87-19877

Contents

1

Seeing the Invisible

In the morning, I see His face
In the evening, His form I trace
In the darkness, His voice I know
I see Jesus everywhere I go.[1]

Seeing the invisible is what I would call the experience of June 6, 1986.

For the past two hours our family had been severely tested and emotionally shaken. Satan's messenger had come on the scene again, trying to bring an untimely death to my dear husband. It was the sixth time he had tried.

Let me take you back to the beginning of the story, which for us began at 4:50 PM June 6, 1986.

I was just driving up our long driveway and met Jim halfway down on his daily jog. We chatted for thirty seconds or so, and he promised to return in one hour for dinner. We would have a relaxed evening with our two overnight guests.

Twenty minutes later I heard the sound of a siren as an emergency vehicle raced down Woodmen Valley Road. I paid scant attention since we often hear sirens in the distance.

I invited our guests to take a short walk with me to see our cabin Jim had built as a cloistered hideaway. We stayed only five minutes and were returning to the

house when I spotted a white van parked in the driveway. It was obvious the two men had found no one
home and were preparing to leave. I shouted and
asked them not to leave, and I broke into a run. As I
reached the driveway the older of the two asked me,
"Is your husband a jogger?" I replied, "Yes." He
didn't need to say more. I could have guessed the rest.
"Did he have on dark blue shorts and no shirt?"
Again, "Yes." "I think he's had a heart attack, and the
ambulance has just taken him to the hospital." Running doubletime, I hit the front porch and cried out to
Jesus to spare my husband.

At the same time I rebuked the spirit of death from
taking him. My next reaction was to call our Bible
study group members; I knew they would immediately
alert the rest of the prayer warriors, and the battle was
on. I also phoned three of our children; none could be
reached. In frustration, I called our neighbor, Gloria
Cruz, and told her to pray, and I left for the hospital.
One of our guests drove me while the other sat in the
backseat praying

My mind began to race crazily to the past and with
it came all the emotions I had felt from his past heart
attacks. There seemed to be no reason for this one and
certainly no warning. Jim had done all in his power to
correct his diet and exercise, and he had been faithful
when others would have grown weary of that life-style.

In twelve minutes we were at the hospital emergency room. It was now 5:40 PM. A nurse, then a doctor,
came out to ask a few questions and tell me even fewer
details. They disappeared again behind a closed door.

A policeman walked up to me and also asked a few questions, giving even fewer details. He had been at the scene of the heart arrest when the ambulance had arrived. I began to add the facts together, and I didn't like what the sum total seemed to be. The dark reality was either a husband who was nearly dead or, at best, severely brain damaged from lack of oxygen. My desire was to be alone. I had already accepted the challenge of spiritual warfare, and I needed to get on with it. I sat in a corner on the floor of the emergency room hallway and continued to do battle with the enemy. I determined the death spirit would *not* have my husband nor would the spirit of brain damage. I was angry at the enemy but at peace with God. How I needed assurance from someone that my darling would be all right. None was forthcoming. The trained emergency staff was battling for his life, also.

By 7:00 PM Jim was moved from the emergency room to the intensive cardiac care unit on the second floor. Presently a nurse came out to tell me that within a few minutes I could see my husband. Certainly, I was anxious to see him and discern for myself the shape he was in. The doctor had pronounced "critical and unstable." I didn't know what that really meant, but it sounded scary.

So many times I had seen Jim in bad shape and hooked up to many tubes and machines. But this time, I was unprepared for what I was about to observe. He was attached to a respirator, and it was breathing for him while he was unconscious. His arms would jerk with involuntary twitches; that was part of the signal he had brain damage. He wasn't functioning on his own.

I walked to his bedside and touched his still, unconscious form. Brushing back his hair with my hand, I began talking softly to him, reminding him he was supposed to be home for dinner. Then I told him he would make it, and I was there to help. We had been through so much together; this was only another hurdle.

Walking out of his room I headed for the bathroom. I hadn't really been alone all day. I also needed to hear from God. Sometimes the bathroom is the only place you can be alone. After splashing cold water on my face I spoke in a quiet voice to my Heavenly Father. "OK, God I need to hear from You. What about this?" In the quietness of my spirit He spoke so reassuringly to me. "My child, he's going to be all right. There are some things I need to teach My servant." With such a knowledge tucked safely into my heart, peace and assurance flooded my soul. I didn't need assurance from a doctor or a nurse anymore. They had told me they couldn't give me a lot of hope anyway. They had seen this type of case nearly every day, and the patient either dies or ends up in a nursing home with his mind gone. I knew neither case would be Jim's destination. He would be sharing the gospel of Jesus Christ once again, and very soon. It was 7:30 PM, June 6, 1986. I had seen the invisible.

Hebrews 11:1 came to mind that "faith is the substance of things hoped for, the evidence of things not seen." I not only hoped, I knew. The knowledge of

Jim's sound mind in the past was all the evidence I needed, even though at the time, he was unconscious and presumed brain damaged from his responses.

I am reminded of that Old Testament saint, Enoch. Hebrews 11:5 says that before God translated Enoch, and took him to heaven without seeing death, "he had this testimony, that he pleased God." Verse 6 tells us how to please God, and that is by living a life of faith. Enoch's life-style was living verse 6.

A life of faith is a life-style, beloved, not something we try out in a time of crisis. If we walk by faith every day, then when a trial arises our faith also arises and will carry us through to victory. Jesus said we are over-whelmingly conquerers. That ought to be enough to fan the flame of faith in your heart and get a bright fire burning.

I encourage you, Christian, to walk that life of faith with Jesus Christ. Then you will know as you walk through the valley of the shadow of death that you are living a life-style pleasing to Him. You, too, will see with the eyes of your spirit. You will be *seeing the invisible.*

1. From "I See Jesus." Words by Thomas O. Chisholm and Music by Harold C. Lowden. Copyright 1917 by Heidelberg Press. © Renewed 1945 by Harold C. Lowden. Assigned to the Rodeheaver Co. (a div. of Word, Inc.). All rights reserved. International Copyright Secured. Used by permission.

2

A Little Billy

Homer was such a funny little fellow when he was six weeks old. His antics kept the family in hilarious laughter and utter frustration. He never failed to let us know when he was hungry and wanted a bottle of formula. He usually followed us around like a little puppy. We truly thought we had a family pet for years to come.

The children were contemplating joining a 4-H club for raising farm animals. Jan wanted a lamb, but in researching what raising a lamb entailed, we found you don't merely raise one. They get lonely, so you raise two. We scratched that idea, and Jan decided she would settle for a goat. We promised to buy one in two weeks for her sixth birthday.

What we knew about goats you could put in a thimble. We knew you milked nannies, so we didn't want one of those. Perhaps a billy goat would do.

We searched the newspaper ads and found someone selling goats. All the children were excited as we piled into the camper and headed out of town toward farm country. We easily found the address and parked the van.

Upon seeing these "wonderful" creatures, Jan squealed with excitement and ran to choose her very own billy goat. He was beautiful with white, long hair, but he wasn't weaned, which meant a bottle several times daily. The owner was asking only eight dollars for him, but I gave her ten. I thought it was an inexpensive amount to make a child so happy. Had I really known what billy goats were all about—I found out six months later—I would have asked her to pay me to take the little rascal off her hands.

The children fell in love with Homer. Whenever my husband Jim went for a jog through the fields, the little goat was running at his heels, enjoying the exercise and companionship. After a few weeks, it was necessary to put him on a leash when Jim ran with him as he began to wander and lag behind. The stubborness in his personality began to become stronger as he grew older. We would walk through the fields with Homer in tow, and suddenly he would stop, sit down, and dig in his heels or leap into the air, doing a somersault while on the end of the tether. He defied us to make him go one inch farther.

His behavior was so incredibly awful that we quit taking him on our walks. We did let him roam the farm at his will. Mostly, he wanted to be with us when we were in the house. One warm evening about dinner time, we left the door open with the screen door latched. Homer wanted in so badly and kept making those "baa-baa" goat sounds. Finally, he took a running start with his head down and crashed right through the screen door into the kitchen. "Baa" again! Seven pairs of eyes stared in amazed unbelief.

He wasn't left to his own devices anymore. We had to keep him chained in the yard to control his behavior. Because this incident involves an animal, it seems amusing. But I've watched the identical behavior in people who profess to be Christians, and that's where it ceases to be funny.

Stubbornness or rebellion left to itself will only bring on pain and destruction and keep us in bondage to the enemy of our souls. In I Samuel 15:23a, God lets us know just how He feels about this behavior. "For rebellion is as the sin of witchcraft, and stubbornness is as iniquity and idolatry."

Rebellion was the original sin in heaven that caused war between Michael, Lucifer, and the angels. A spirit of rebellion exalts ourselves above the Most High God. The attitude of rebellion is really saying, "I shall reserve for myself the right to make the final decision." That, beloved, is the very reason Lucifer and one third of the angels in heaven were cast down to this earth.

That same decision is why Adam and Eve were driven from their perfect earthly home. They made the decision to usurp God's work by rebelling and thereby broke the oneness between God and man. That broken oneness could only be made whole again through a blood sacrifice. Jesus' death on the cross was the sacrifice required by God for the atonement. Perhaps we can catch a glimpse and understand why rebellion and stubbornness are as witchcraft and idolatry to God. It cost Him everything!

We are like the billy goat in only one way—behavior. We don't have an excuse of an animal's mind; we have the mind of Christ. All we need is a desire to live in obedience to the will of God.

If rebellion and stubbornness have been plaguing you, confess it like any other sin and have a contrite heart about it. God, through His Holy Spirit, can teach any contrite, willing heart how to obey. Then we will find contentment, letting God make the final decisions and having the last word.

"For it is God who is at work in you, both to will and to work for His good pleasure" (Phil. 2:13, NASB).

3

Wrong Decisions

Summers in Walla Walla, Washington, where I grew up, could be unbearably hot. I think we must have lived there before the days of air conditioners. Anyway, we didn't know a soul who owned one.

In the heat of summer, July and August, it's *always* canning time in that part of the country. With all the stove burners turned on high, the kitchen becomes as hot as a boiler factory.

This particular hot day I'd had it with the heat in the kitchen, I had mopped my brow for the last time and went in search for an electric fan. I knew Dad kept one in the garage and soon I found it. It was so dusty with dirt and grime I felt surely it must need a good dose of some exotic oil to keep the motor running in perfect order.

My teenage eyes searched Dad's workshop for the lubricating oil. Try as I might, I couldn't remember if it was called "3 in 1," "4 in 1," or "5 in 1." I knew it was called one of those, but no oilcan with that name was in sight. My eyes spotted a can; ah, this must be it. I took down a half-gallon tin with bold letters, LIN-

SEED OIL, and proceeded to slop it over all moving parts. Finding an old paint rag, I wiped off the excess oil and carried the fan into the house.

The whirring blades were running ever so quietly, and I was pleased with myself. The moving blades didn't make the kitchen any cooler; instead it circulated the hot air. The fan ran all afternoon just perfectly, but as time came for my Dad to return home from work, the blades seemed to turn a little slower. *It must be tired, just like I am,* I thought.

When Dad came in the door, he saw the fan running at slow speed and wondered aloud if anyone had bothered to oil it. "Oh, sure, Dad," I piped up, "I did." "I couldn't find the one you usually use so I tried a different kind from your paint shelf. It's linseed oil."

If I live to be one hundred, I'll never forget the pained look on his face. His hand flew to his forehead and from his throat came a low moan. Oh, oh, I knew I had done something wrong.

"Baby, you never, never oil any machinery with linseed oil. It gets sticky, and on a hot motor the oil gets real gummy. Then the motor stops, and all is ruined." Dad had explained this to me with such love and patience it made me feel all the worse for doing the wrong thing for the right reason. I think it took him several hours to correct the mess I had made, but he never complained or condemned me.

I am reminded of another person who did the wrong thing for the right reason.

We read in the Book of Exodus (17:6) where God specifically told Moses and the elders of Israel to lead

His Chosen People to a certain rock. God instructed Moses to hit it with his rod. Water gushed forth for the complaining, thirsty Hebrews and all their cattle.

Some years later we come upon the same scene. You'd think after nearly forty years wandering in the desert, God's Chosen People, living like nomads, would have learned to trust Him and live by faith. Not so! They never did learn the vital lesson of walking by faith. Instead they always lived by "Show me, and I'll believe." They murmured, they complained, they had great pity parties and feasted on unbelief. No wonder Moses was at the end of his patience with several million of God's chosen.

In Numbers 20:7-12, we read a sad story of Moses doing the wrong thing for the right reason.

The Israelites were now in sight of the hills of Canaan; a few more days of traveling would bring them to the borders of the land which God had promised them. Even though their water supply had ended, they were near Edom where God instructed Moses to buy food and water for the people. Edom was on the road to Canaan. They should have realized that just around the corner was plenty of food and water and willingly walked the rest of the road by faith. Faith in God was not uppermost in their thoughts; thirst was. Their cries and complaints were directed against Moses and Aaron. Would they ever go to the Source for Him to meet their needs?

Moses and Aaron sought the face of God for direction once again, and God instructed them.

> Take the rod and you and your brother Aaron assemble
> the congregation and speak to the rock before their eyes,
> that it may yield its water. You shall thus bring forth
> water for them out of the rock and let the congregation
> and their beasts drink (Num. 20:8, NASB).

Long had Moses and Aaron borne the rebellion and
obstinance of Israel; now, at last, Moses' patience gave
way to wrath. He spoke in a loud voice to those assem-
bled at the rock, "Listen now, you rebels; shall we
bring forth water for you out of this rock?" (v.10,
NASB).

Moses' lack of self-control and patience was evident
as he lifted up his rod and struck the rock twice. Water
gushed forth. God had said, *Speak* to the rock";
Moses' anger said, *"hit."* He had offended God; he
had not obeyed.

Moses' impetuous sin shattered the lesson God
desired to teach the children of Israel. Many commen-
tators have believed the rock was indeed a symbol of
Christ. I heartily agree. The rock had been struck once.
Twice disagreed with God's economy. The rock was to
be struck only once; Christ was to be offered only
once. What a picture.

The second time, all Moses had to do was speak to
the rock, even as we are to ask for blessings in the holy
name of Jesus. What a tragedy it was that Moses yield-
ed to impatience and tried to force the bountiful hand
of God. We are never to demand of Him—only to ask
in Jesus' name. God was dishonored before the children of Israel, rather than glorified and magnified.

Even though Moses could have excused his sin with,

"Lord, I am worn-out; I have heavy burdens upon me; These people have taxed my endurance," he could not excuse himself for such headstrong disobedience.

Even though we have been loyal and true in the past, that does not bypass current disobedience. As the expression goes, "The bigger they are, the harder they fall." The more responsibility, the more accountability. Failure through willful disobedience then calls for heavier punishment.

For this one act of doing the wrong thing for the right reason, Moses and Aaron were later denied entrance into the blessed Promised Land. They could only view the land from afar, and they died before they were able to realize the fulfillment of God's promises to His chosen people.

Leaders of God's people, watch out. Walk in the light. Stay close to Christ. Walk not in the flesh but in the Spirit. "Judgment begins at the house of God." Satan attacks us at our weak points, but we can be overcomers through Him that loves us.

God promises help for us, no matter how difficult and trying the circumstances. Through His power we may conquer. "Onward Christian Soldiers!"

4

By the Waterfront

Come with me by the waterfront and turn your time clock back fifteen years. Of course, you must be invisible not to disturb my aloneness.

It is Sunday afternoon, and the waterfront is quiet from the daily hustle and bustle. We hear the cry of the seagulls as they fly over the water searching for food. You'll hear the faint creaking of the moored shrimp boats as the gentle wind lulls them to sleep. Do you smell what I smell? Yes, that's the creosote painted on the pilings to preserve them from rot. You say the water is murky? Yes, I know the water isn't clear, but then it never is here. The pollution does make one sad.

Let's find a place to sit so I can put these pencils to work on the sketch pad I am carrying. See that log over there? Let's sit on that one.

It's really too bad the day is so bright and warm and I am so sad. I don't want to be sad. I am sad because I cannot find any answers in my search for a relationship with God. I feel empty, like an old, dusty, dry well. Lonely? Oh, sure, and it makes me shiver. It feels like isolation on a floating iceberg. Is there nothing to stop the hurting or to fill the vacuum? The questions come fast and furious. Why am I here? Where am I going? No answers; just more questions.

I keep aimlessly sketching first one piece of trash at my feet and then another. I begin to draw an old weather-beaten board. The wind spins a broken white plastic cup in front of my feet. "Stop the world; I want to get off."

I'm crying out loud to God—shouting in the wind, "This is just like my life, trash blowing in the wind. God, help me, I just can't do it myself anymore." I am tired; I am drained. Tears are coming so copiously they are dripping off my chin.

I'm sorry. I didn't mean to embarrass you with my tears, but I've been crying a lot lately.

In a flash, the tears stop. I see something, do you? Oh, of course not, it's in my head or is it my spirit? A boxing ring emerges. Two people are in the arena. I recognize them both—Jesus and Satan. The battle is quick and intense. I know it's for my soul. Then it stops as quickly as it started. There is a victor. Jesus comes into the center of the ring with His arm of victory held high. He had fought the devil for my soul and won. I was His prize; I belonged to Him.

Overwhelming peace is flooding my body, mind, and spirit. Can you tell? You'll see. It is real.

I think it's time to go home now. Thank you for coming with me and sharing the most important day of my life. Today I met *Him,* and I'm different.

Many years later I was looking through some of my old yellowed drawings, and I came upon the one I had sketched that day by the waterfront. How could I have missed the significance of that old weather-beaten board? It was rough and had an old, rusty nail protruding from a worn hole. It had the word *UP* boldly stamped in red ink and a black arrow pointing heavenward.

As I studied that drawing, tears welled up in my eyes. The memories came flooding back, and I could remember every detail as though it were yesterday. God had not only given a vision, but He had sent a printed sign. I had missed it.

As I consider the impact of that old board, I am reminded of the lyrics to that precious hymn, "The Old Rugged Cross."

> On a hill far away stood an old rugged cross,
> The emblem of suff'ring and shame;
> And I love that old cross where the dearest and best
> For a world of lost sinners was slain.
> So I'll cherish the old rugged cross
> Till my trophies at last I lay down;
> I will cling to the old rugged cross,
> And exchange it some day for a crown.

5

Blessed Unity

Every spring the magnificent mountain bluebirds come back to the Irwins, just like the swallows return to Capistrano, California. They come to find suitable housing for raising a family.

"The male in breeding finery is all turquoise blue. Flashing through the air, swooping or hovering over my garden on rapidly beating wings, he seems like a living model for the beautiful turquoise jewelry fashioned by some of the western Indians."[1]

We always see the male first, since he has the responsibility of house hunting. Jim has erected several homemade houses near the garden for the couples to choose from. Mr. Bluebird thoroughly checks out the heating, cooling, drainage, the roof, and the general stability of the construction. He then returns with the Mrs. and the conversation probably goes something like this.

"My dear, don't you think this will be a lovely, quiet cottage to raise our family?"

"Perhaps," she chirps, "I do like it, and it's the best we've seen so far."

He twitters back, "We'll return tomorow and make our decision after we have slept on the idea." She is in agreement. As they fly off toward their temporary living quarters, I hear them twittering something about being close to the grocery store and a good place for the children's flying lessons.

I knew they would return in the morning and move in. They always do. They were there, and they had moved in.

In no time at all they had built a sturdy nest in the nursery and lined it with soft fluff. Now it was ready for the five or six eggs she would lay. From then on one or the other would sit on the eggs to keep them warm until they hatched. While one sat, the other hunted for food or perched close by. Often one would bring the egg sitter a juicy bug for a snack. I had rarely seen such consideration among birds.

Never had I seen a busier couple than Mr. and Mrs. Bluebird. You always know when their babies hatch since the size of their brood keeps them both on the hunt for food.

Fortunately for them, their house is at my garden— hence many creepy crawlers for empty stomachs. When a parent flies to the doorway with a tender morsel, all the young ones begin to chorus, "Me next." This goes on for weeks from dawn until dusk.

As I work in my garden and observe this delightful little family, I feel like a curious neighbor with a nose glued to a window. They are so fascinating I just can't quit watching. I learn a lot about people by watching little and big creatures. Only one thing disappoints me—I've never seen the baby birds take flying lessons. One day they are yelling for more food, the next everyone is gone.

After a short vacation, maybe a few weeks, the bluebirds return to their summer home to start a second family. Talk about busy!

How often, as I've watched them, I've thought about God's word concerning the responsibility of husbands to wives and wives to husbands.

The Creator saw it was not good for a man to be alone so He made him a helper that was suitable for him (see Gen. 2:18). God created her from one of Adam's ribs, therefore the husband is to cleave to his wife, and they shall become one flesh. To cleave means to adhere closely, stick by, cling to, to remain faithful. Their bodies, minds, and spirits become one. How wonderful to know that God provides a special oneness between husband and wife which must never be shared with anyone else.

The apostle Peter reminds wives to have a gentle and meek spirit as they submit to their husbands (see 1 Pet. 3:4-5). This admirable quality in a woman is precious in the sight of God because it costs her something. It costs her loving obedience to the Word of God.

Watchman Nee, in *The Release of the Spirit*, expresses the quality of meekness this way. "One broken by the Spirit naturally possesses meekness. His contacts with people are no longer marked by that obstinacy, hardness and sharpness which are the hallmarks of an unbroken man. He has been brought to the place where his attitude is as meek as his voice is gentle. The fear of God in his heart naturally finds expression in his words and manner."

To husbands the apostle Peter says, ". . . live with your wives in an understanding way, as with a weaker vessel, since she is a woman; and grant her honor as a fellow heir of the grace of life, so that your prayers may not be hindered" (1 Pet. 3:7, NASB).

Husband and wife must work together for the common good of the marriage and the family. That means caring and sharing. Just like the bluebirds working together in unity to raise their young ones until they leave the nest, married couples, too, need to stay in the spirit of unity, sharing their joys and problems together. Caring enough to be involved with the other mate's life means to want God's very best for both of them. The time invested to create a spirit of unity pays great dividends.

Does it sound like too pat an answer, just too much work to achieve, or downright impossible? God doesn't think so. You can live in unity and harmony if that desire is your goal. You can say as did the apostle Paul, "I can do all things through Christ which strengtheneth me" (Phil. 4:13).

1. Alexander Wetmore, *Song and Garden Birds of North America* (New York: National Geographic Society, n.d.), p. 220.

6

Turn On the Light

Most of us at one time or another have visited a cave while on summer vacation. The coolness inside is such a wonderful respite from the soaring summer temperatures.

One year our family visited Carlsbad Caverns in New Mexico. The children were fascinated with the bats which hung upside down just inside the mouth of the cave. Most of all, they wanted to touch the beautiful stalagmite and stalactite formations which looked like a fairyland when lighted.

Another year we visited Cave of the Winds in Manitou Springs, Colorado. The temperature inside the cave is cool and steady all year round. The complete darkness is also the same year round. Our young guide carried a lantern as she led us into the bowels of the earth through narrow, winding passageways. Soon, before us loomed a gigantic, yawning cavern. Everyone stopped as she began to explain details concerning the wind, temperature, and such. At one point she turned out the light so we could see how black and empty was the darkness. She told us to put our hands in front of our faces; everyone dutifully obeyed. The guide was right; you couldn't even see your hand without the benefit of a light. She also said if a person spent very many days in the cave without any light, they would go blind. What a terrible thought.

Now, just suppose the tourists inside the cave decided they didn't need any help or any light to find their way back to the entrance and dismissed the guide with curtness. Hypothetical? Maybe. Preposterous, no!

It happens every day to millions of people in this old wicked world. They have chosen to make that very decision for their life-style. They say, "I don't need a guide, I'll guide myself. I don't need a light, I know exactly where I'm going and what I'm doing." Do they? Of course not. They have chosen the darkness rather than the light. Why? The Bible tells us why.

> And this is the judgment, that the light is come into the world, and men loved the darkness rather than the light; for their deeds were evil. For everyone who does evil hates the light, . . . lest his deeds should be exposed (John 3:19-20, NASB).

Foolish people, God says He's going to expose the evil deeds anyway. Nothing is hidden from God. Those who choose to reject "The Light" of the world, Jesus, and prefer the darkness have chosen to serve the devil. He becomes their master. They do not realize how dark is their darkness. "The lamp of the body is the eye; if therefore, your eye is clear your whole body will be full of light. But if your eye is bad, your whole body will be full of darkness. If therefore, the light that is in you is darkness, how great is the darkness!'' (Matt. 6:22-23, NASB).

If you, dear reader, are in that condition today, my heart cries out to you. Don't be sucked into the eternal darkness of Satan. Come into the Light and let Jesus cleanse you. Let the Holy Spirit turn the spotlight on those dark areas of sin and reveal them to you. You will never want to walk in darkness again.

If you are born again, I say to you, our task is to be that light upon a hill—a light that shines so brightly with the glory of God it cannot be hidden and will expose the vast expanse of emptiness, loneliness, and blackness. Hold the torch high as you march under the banner of the cross, for soon you shall hear the words of the Holy One:

> He that is unjust, let him be unjust still; and he which is filthy, let him be filthy still; and he that is righteous, let him be righteous still: and he that is holy, let him be holy still. And behold I come quickly; and my reward is with me, to give every man according as his work shall be (Rev. 22:11-12).

7

Lost

Jan was about ten years old when she went on a speaking trip to Omaha, Nebraska, with her daddy. Oh, how the children cherish these times alone with their father.

This time Jim had several people traveling with him. They had just signed the hotel register and were given keys to their separate rooms. Jan would stay with her dad. He gave her one key and told her he would meet her in their room in a few moments. Feeling very grown up, she entered the elevator and pushed the third floor button. From there she seemed to evaporate.

Jim finished some important details of his speaking engagement and headed up to the room. He turned the key in the lock and called, "Jan." No Jan. Perhaps she was checking out the swimming pool or the restaurant. Maybe she had gone down the hall to the cold drink machine or the ice maker. Time passed. One hour, two hours. Where was his daughter? She had never been away this long without her daddy's consent. Panic began to set in. It just wasn't like Jan to wander off in strange places.

Jim called the rooms of those traveling with him. No, they had not seen Jan. They would start looking. He alerted the hotel that his child was missing and to keep an eye out for her. The hotel security joined the search party. More time passed. Jim and the rest of the group knocked on all the doors in the hotel, often awakening people from their sleep. There were eight floors.

Jim reluctantly called me to share the frightening news, all the while hoping I wouldn't panic. Panic, are you kidding? Fear gripped me, and I felt sick inside. I must have had a dozen questions in my mind. Most of all, I was hoping she would not be afraid of the unknown. In utter, helpless despair, I cried out to God, "Please protect my little girl from the evil one. Please don't let her be afraid," and on I wailed in the darkness. Finally, I shut up and became quiet on the inside. At that moment, something wonderful happened. God spoke to my heart so loudly I thought it was audible. I saw with my spirit His overwhelming greatness. He spoke the words, "I Am that I Am" (Ex. 3:14).

Indelibly awed—for I shall never forget it—I was aware of my infinite smallness and His infinite greatness. Immediate peace flooded my soul. I knew wherever Jan was, God was. Whatever she was doing, He saw and had His protecting hand over her. All fear left.

I went to bed and fell asleep. A few hours (or was it moments?) later I was awakened by the jangling of the telephone. Jim was on the other end to tell me the good news. Jan had been found. How it all happened still has us puzzled to this day. Jan was waiting for her daddy behind the door of the only room which had not been searched.

Jan had misread the room number, but her key fit the door on the same floor. She went in and flopped down on the bed to wait for her dad. Becoming bored, she turned on the television to pass the time. After several hours she tired of waiting and decided to go looking for her father. She came face to face with one of the group members who had been looking for her. "Where have you been?" The question seemed foolish to Jan. "Where's my dad?" was her reply. She was tearfully hugged and taken to her dad.

I am reminded of the parable Jesus taught in Luke 15:4-7 of the one lost sheep. The shepherd left the ninety-nine sheep in the field and went searching for the lost one. He didn't quit looking until he found the sheep. Friend, no matter how lost you are, Jesus is out searching for you. He's knocking on all the hotel doors looking for His lost child. In your pain you may entertain the question, "God, where are you?" He is there all the time. Where are you? Are you that one lost sheep?

When you eventually find one another, there may be tearful hugs; but I can assure you, all heaven rejoices when a lost one comes home.

8

Bearing Fruit

Weeds, weeds, weeds! Just looking at my vegetable garden I had planted a month earlier made me feel depressed. Since the garden measures approximately 48' x 66', I mentally assessed the time required to clear out the mess. "It will take at least a month," I groaned. *Why do I always take an overseas trip with my husband during the months of June or July? The garden is always a disaster when I return.*

Well, just go down there and get started, I told myself the very next day. Kneeling down and bending low I searched for the tiny plants amoung the nearly two-feet-tall weeds. Carefully, carefully I weeded around the tender shoots. Sometimes I accidently pulled up the little vegetable plants because of the denseness of the weeds. In many cases the weeds had taken over completely and choked out my new seedlings. The weeds were tall, thick, and a lush green; but my corn plants looked anemic. The weeds had sapped the water and nutrients from the earth, leaving the vegetables malnourished, weak, and nearly dead. After weeding some of the anemic plants they withered and died when the heat from the sun beat down on them.

I tenderly cared for the little plants, knowing full well they would bear good fruit. It would require plenty of my time, patience, and daily watering, but it was more than worth the time spent in labor. It also gave me precious time to be alone with Jesus to talk with Him and listen to His voice.

My garden is organic with a heavy layer of compost and is very fertile. Because of the plussage we have lovely vegetables every summer to freeze for the winter and an abundance to share with family and friends.

Jesus told a parable about the sower and his seed in Luke 8:5-15. A sower went out and planted his seed by broadcasting. That is, he threw it helter-skelter. That's OK for wheat farming or planting a lawn; that is not OK for gardens. Some of the seed fell by the way and the birds ate it. Some fell among the rocks. As soon as it took root and sprang through the earth, it withered away for lack of water, too many rocks, and not enough soil. Some seeds fell among the thorns, and as they grew together the weeds choked the wheat. Other seed fell on the fertile soil, sprang up, and bore fruit one hundredfold.

This example reminded me of my own garden. The seeds I had planted represented the Word of God. The seeds I had planted in a small area of my garden with many pebbles reflected people which hear and receive the Word gladly, but because of too many rocks and not enough soil, there is no stability for a deep root system. They give intellectual assent for awhile but in the heat of the sun they shrivel spiritually.

Those seeds that were planted and the weeds that took over are an example of those who hear God's Word and go forth but are choked with the worries, riches, and pleasures of this life. They worry about all the work they must accomplish. They worry about all the money they need to take care of their wants, desires, and needs. After they have their money they worry about how to keep it from the Internal Revenue Service.

Then comes a day off or a week's vacation, no time for the Word then; after all, a person needs some pleasures to get his mind off his worries. These are they which have choked out the Word of God from their lives and do not bring any spiritual fruit to maturity.

The seeds I plant in rows or hills and keep weed-free and watered are like those who hear the Word and keep it with an honest and good heart. They hold fast to God's Word and bear fruit for Him one hundred-fold.

Let us receive God's Word with joy and develop a profound root system to keep us standing firm and straight during the time of testing. Let us get rid of all the weeds and never be choked with the worries of this world. Peter said, "Casting all your care upon him; for he careth for you" (1 Pet. 5:7). Leave your cares with Jesus and concentrate on bearing fruit one hundred-fold for His kingdom.

9

Caleb the Perfect— Molly the Rogue

Caleb is a beautiful, red-haired Irish Setter. He has all the markings of a pedigree; unfortunately he has no papers.

Caleb was found wandering the streets several years ago, and every effort was made to find the owner. Ads were placed in all the local papers, and notices were tacked in conspicuous places. The owner was not to be found, so Ty look the dog home and became his new master.

It was obvious from day one that someone had really loved and cared for this animal because he was super obedient. If Ty would tell the dog to sit and stay, he could be sure Caleb would be sitting in the same place many hours later. If he was left in the house for long periods of time, he would rather burst then make a mess. I've never seen such an obedient dog, that is, until he met Molly. But I'm getting ahead of the story.

If Caleb was at the top of the canine list, Molly was at the bottom for having class. She was a "Heinz 57" variety, stray, and certainly no lady. It was visible she had been severely mistreated. Often she cowered or hid. Ty took her home, too.

She was, without a doubt, the very opposite of Caleb in every way. She would run away and not come home for hours. Caleb stayed within a twenty-five foot radius of the house. This was amazing, considering the family lived on twenty acres.

One day Ty's mother was sitting on the deck sipping a cup of coffee while watching the two dogs. The episode that unfolded simply astounded her.

Caleb was sitting, minding his own business; but Molly had an itch for wandering. She wanted company on her forthcoming adventure. Her female power shifted into high gear. She came up and nuzzled him, then headed down the lane. After a few yards she stopped, turned around, and saw he had not followed. Returning to him she repeated her feminine nuzzling, then marched off toward the unknown. He looked longingly after her. She stopped again and turned around. Again, he had not followed. He pointed his nose in the opposite direction, pretending not to notice. She returned to his side, whined, and nuzzled him again. Setting her chin high, she sallied forth, expecting him to follow. He watched desirously until she stopped and turned around. Finally Caleb could no longer withstand the temptation and trotted off with her.

In less than half an hour Molly's undisciplined influence ruined many years of loving obedience. He hasn't stayed home since and is often gone overnight.

When Ty's mother told me this story, I couldn't help

thinking of Scripture. Solomon wrote in Proverbs 1:-10,15, "My son, if sinners entice you, Do not consent. My son, do not walk in the way with them. Keep your feet from their path" (NASB).

In Proverbs 4:14-16 Solomon repeated this godly advice. "Do not enter the path of the wicked, And do not proceed in the way of evil men. Avoid it, do not pass by it; Turn away from it and pass on. For they cannot sleep unless they do evil; And they are robbed of sleep unless they make someone stumble" (NASB).

What straightforward words of counsel, but all too often disregarded! Disobedience will ultimately be punished in the lake of fire that God has prepared for the devil and his angels.

God has called His children to a life of obedience. Either we obey and make Him Lord in our lives, or He is not Lord at all. If He is not Lord, we too will find ourselves enticed to sin and follow the ungodly ones down the wide path to destruction.

Caleb is still a loving dog, but his character is ruined. Unlike Caleb, we have a Savior who forgives us when we confess our sins; therefore, our character is not ruined. He still trusts us to make the right decision.

The choice is ours, and Jesus will help. He will not allow us to be tempted beyond what we are able to bear and with that temptation He will provide a way for us to escape (see 1 Cor. 10:13). Thank you, Jesus, we are more than conquerers; we do not have to yield to temptation.

How about it, Christians? The challenge is ours. Will we obey God when no one is around to check up?

10

Sirocco

A dear older couple was over for dinner one Sunday evening after church. When the meal was finished, we just sat around the table visiting. The older gentleman had been raised on a huge farm in Lamar, Colorado. The soil is very fertile, but the summer temperatures can become unbearably hot, dry, windy, and dusty. He had just made a remark about seeing a fence post fall over by itself one time.

I teased him, thinking we were about to hear one of his funny jokes. Instead, he became very serious. The type of fence post he was talking about had been sunk nearly two feet into the ground, leaving almost four feet above ground.

He said he had watched a steady wind blow for weeks without a letup. As the wind blew, he observed the soil around the fence post and noticed it was beginning to erode little by little, day by day. Every few days, he'd look again, and more and more of the fence was exposed.

Day after day the wind continued to blow. Deeper and deeper grew the depression until nearly all of the post was visible. One day the post just fell down. Its struggle to stand erect was over.

The room grew very quiet. I was absorbing what I had heard. Suddenly my mouth gaped as I explained to our daughter Jill, "That's just like relationships with people. That's like some marriages I know." The analogy of the story profoundly affected me.

I have heard married couples sniping at one another with catty remarks designed to hurt only a little at a time. After years of hurting a little bit at a time, the very foundation of their marriage had crumbled and fallen. The love and trust had eroded. The wind of biting words had blown far too long and, like the fence post, the struggle to stand was over. God's principles of marriage had been violated. Love and respect had wafted away like a fluffy, white cloud and left a residue of dryness and bitterness in the soul. Submitting to each other as unto the Lord hadn't even been considered in the relationship.

Paul wrote in Ephesians 5:33: "Nevertheless let each individual among you also love his own wife even as himself; and let the wife see to it that she respect her husband" (NASB).

Jesus said, ". . . for out of the abundance of the heart the mouth speaketh" (Matt. 12:34). If it's not in the heart, it won't be in the mouth.

Perhaps the secret to turning around a stormy marriage is for God to change our hearts. When the heart is pure the mouth also follows in purity.

When we are willing to follow God's guidelines for our marriages, they will not be fraught with unkindness, bitter words, and boundless pain. They will be filled with the very essence of love, respect, and oneness in the Spirit. They will be filled with the fruit of the Spirit (see Gal. 5:22-23).

David of old prayed, "Create in me a clean heart, O God; and renew a right spirit within me" (Ps. 51:10).

Will you pray that prayer today from the depths of your heart so your marriage will be a glory to God? It may be difficult, but with God, all things are possible to those who believe.

He can and will make your marriage a blessing to you and an example to those who are watching. He delights in making Christian marriages strong. A three-ply cord cannot easily be broken. You, your mate, and Jesus can make a strong, permanent bond that will be a glory to God and a blessing to others.

11

Counting the Cost

Russia. To millions that name means home. For countless others it means fear, loss of freedom, or perhaps death. To the world traveler it may mean a new, exotic place to visit and buy some unique souvenirs. To me it was fear of the unknown because of the horror stories I had heard or read.

When Jim came home from the office one day with an exciting invitation to preach in the Soviet Union, I was none too excited to go. Obediently, I applied for a visa, all the while hoping it would never arrive. After all, we had five children at home, and they needed their mother there, not off somewhere in jail in a foreign land. The devil had a heyday with my mind.

My visa arrived on schedule, so I dragged out my suitcase and began to pack. A few days later we were winging our way to Russia, for me the unknown. What God had in store for us, I never could have guessed. Would I be frightened out of my wits by gun-toting soldiers, or would I see the infamous KGB agents following us?

After nearly twenty-four hours of flying, our very

fatigued group of ten arrived in Russia. We were met by a small group of born-again Christian believers, bearing flowers. Our host, who had invited us, was not there to meet us. We were informed that pastor Joseph Bondarinko was in a prison for preaching to a youth group, even though he had obtained the needed permission. That bit of information was a little unsettling; and we were saddened.

When one arrives in the USSR the officials know of your whereabouts nearly every second through their official "Intourist" travel agency. (It's probably nothing more than an arm of the KGB-secret police.) Upon checking into your hotel, the desk clerk confiscates your passport, and you don't see it again until you check out. This action certainly unnerved me. Many of their moves may cause fear to spring up in the heart.

The United States State Department warned us that our hotel rooms and taxis would probably be bugged with listening devices. While praying in our room, I made sure I prayed long and loud just in case they were listening. Whenever we needed to communicate plans or feelings it was either in a low whisper or written on a piece of paper which was then torn to small bits and flushed down the toilet.

How well I remember seeing many KGB agents. It became a game of intrigue for me. I don't know who trained them, but to me they were so obvious it became funny. Often I would wave to them just to watch their expressions. Sometimes I'd watch as they pretended to be busy or hide, much to their chagrin.

Jim was convinced I was imagining things. Imagination or not, I was looking for them with amused fascination.

The best times of all were with the "believers." The Russian Christians call themselves "believers." They were the *only* happy people we saw. Their salvation and their love for Jesus were about all they had to be happy about. They invited us into their homes and gave us large meals and small gifts. We knew they were poor financially, but they gave to us out of their poverty! It was humbling enough to make the tough cry.

Speaking in the registered churches was such a peaceful joy. We knew the KGB agents were in the meetings, too, taking notes; not on the sermon, but as to who attended. They would use the information at a later time to persecute the Christians. We saw only a few people come forward in the churches to accept Jesus as their Savior. They knew the high price they must pay; they had counted the cost. New Christians knew they would be removed from a good job to a street-sweeping one or, if a student in the university, expelled from school and all records destroyed.

In the eyes of the government, Christians become nonpeople. In the registered churches you mostly find older people and a few young marrieds. In the underground churches (the unregistered) is where you find all the enthusiastic young people. They are there because the government tries to regulate the Christian home. It tells them they cannot teach their children Christian principles or about God until they are eighteen years old. If that family goes to a registered church they must sign a document promising not to teach their children what the government has forbidden. Those godly people won't prostitute themselves by signing such documents, so they attend the unregistered underground churches. Sometimes those churches meet in the forest, winter and summer, or in clandestine places, and occasionally in a believer's home.

One day, while ministering in one of the churches, we were asked a very pointed question by one of the members. "What do you have to give up in America to become a Christian?" We were taken totally off guard; that question had never been asked us before. We didn't have a ready answer. A feeling of shame crept over us, for we knew we didn't have to give up the things they were asked to give up when they accepted Jesus as Savior. It was difficult to know how to react to such a question.

Later, as I reflected on the question, I knew the answer. God expects the same thing from all of His children. Allow me to quote Jesus, from Matthew 10:32-39. "If anyone publicly acknowledges me as his friend, I will openly acknowledge him as my friend before my father in heaven. But if anyone publicly denies me, I will openly deny him before my Father in heaven. Don't imagine that I came to bring peace to the earth! No, rather, a sword. I have come to set a man against his father, and a daughter against her mother, and a daughter-in-law against her mother-in-law—a man's worst enemies will be right in his own home! If you love your father and mother more than you love me, you are not worthy of being mine; or if you love your son or daughter more than me, you are not worthy of being mine. If you refuse to take up your cross and follow me, you are not worthy of being mine. If you cling to your life, you will lose it; but if you give it up for me, you will save it" (TLB).

Christ's mission, as well as ours for Him, involves tension, persecution, and death. Not that this is our desire, but in conforming to His image and serving Him, we are guaranteed these problems. The gospel divides some families, simply because some choose to follow Jesus and others don't have the same desire. Two cannot walk together unless they be agreed; and a house divided against itself will fall.

What do we have to give up in America to follow Jesus? Regardless of our race or country of birth, Jesus' requirement for all of us is exactly the same. We must give up everything and everyone that stand between us and following Him. We all must take up our cross of self-denial and follow Him.

12

My Sermon

One and a half miles from our home is a newly closed road. Some of the neighbors have decided to turn it into a used-car lot. On weekends that area has many cars for sale.

While driving home the other day, I noticed a boat had joined the "For Sale" group. The name emblazoned on its smooth white side caught my attention. *My Sermon* it said. *My Sermon,* I mumbled to myself, a question mark rising in my head. "What a strange name for a boat," I remarked to my husband. "Why would anyone name their boat, *My Sermon?* I must be missing the meaning, Honey, what do you think it means?" I persisted. I just didn't understand. Jumping to conclusions, I thought, *It probably means the owner is using the boat as an excuse for not attending church.* Mulling the thought over in my mind, the name seemed so unappropriate and, at the same time, probably an honest feeling of the owner.

If it was such a wonderful substitute for being in church and hearing the Word of God, why were they selling it? I couldn't answer my own question; but I did think of several verses of Scripture I wanted to beat them over the head with. "For they all seek after their own interests, not those of Christ Jesus" (Phil. 2:21, NASB). Those who seek after the ways of the world, not only seek after their own interests, but they have no inclination toward going to church or the things of God. Nor do they want anything to do with God.

I wrote another page to finish this story, but my spirit was unsettled about it. Something was wrong. A nagging feeling kept after me until I decided to dial the phone number that was printed on the "For Sale" sign.

A male voice answered. I told him who I was and that I had written a story about his boat. He seemed interested and willing to share the reason for selling. Then he dropped the bomb! He was a preacher. He had just moved his family to town and was preparing to start a new church; and since we have no lakes close by for sailing, he didn't need his boat.

Then I asked a question I almost wished I hadn't. "Why did you call your boat *My Sermon?*" A chuckle came over the other end of the wire as he explained. It had been his release from pressures. His hobby. If one of his church members called his home and wished to speak with him they would inquire of his wife if he was working on his sermon. If so, they did not wish to disturb him. It got to be such a joke, especially if he was working on his boat, that he decided to name his boat *My Sermon.*

As I stood, holding the phone, suddenly I had a very dry throat and a very red face. I croaked out a thank-you, mumbled a few other words of embarrassment, and hung up. I knew I needed to change this story. I had judged my brother wrongly and had based my conclusions totally on what I thought, not on the facts. No wonder my spirit was unsettled with the story I had written. Shame flooded me as I was chastened by the Holy Spirit. Repentance was forthcoming, as was confession to the Lord. The Holy Spirit burned Matthew 7:1-2 deep into my heart. "Do not judge lest you be judged. For in the way you judge, you will be judged; and by your standard of measure, it will be measured to you" (NASB).

I believe God's message is very, very clear and needs no further explanation. I was wrong and needed to be corrected. He taught me another valuable lesson and, in so doing, spared me a lot of embarrassment from future temptations to judge another. God is so long-suffering with His children and loves us too much to leave us like we are.

The Letter to the Hebrews (12:5-6) teaches: "My son, do not regard lightly the discipline of the Lord, Nor faint when you are reproved by Him; For those whom the Lord loves He disciplines, and He scourges every son whom He receives" (NASB).

I'm so glad He corrected me that day concerning judging others and set me on a straightened course. I'm a fast learner; I find it hurts too much when I keep repeating a sin and then am chastened by the Lord.

13

The Lady with the Lamp

In New York's harbor stands a proud, elderly lady. She is one hundred years old. In her right hand she holds a torch heavenward and cradles in her left arm a tablet representing the Declaration of Independence. She never grows fatigued but remains faithfully erect year after year. You will never hear her speak audibly, but all strangers and friends know her voice and hear her message. She represents liberty freed from her chains. We know her as the *Statute of Liberty.*

The massive statute was placed in the harbor on October 28, 1886. It was a gift from the country of France as a memorial to French and American friendship and to celebrate the centenary of America's independence.

She was to be a reminder of freedom to all those who saw her, whether Americans or strangers from a foreign soil. With loving, open arms, she welcomes and receives all those who come to America.

A beautiful poem is engraved on Liberty's pedestal by Emma Lazarus. We are most familiar with the last part of the poem. The words have even been set to music and echo the very heartbeat of our country.

> Give me your tired, your poor,
> Your huddled masses yearning to breathe free,
> The wretched refuse of your teeming shore.
> Send these, the homeless tempest-tost to me,
> I lift my lamp beside the golden door

Thousands of refugees have wept silently when they first viewed "The Lady with the Lamp" as they sailed into New York harbor. They were hanging all their dreams, their hopes, their desires on the meaning of this statue like one would hang clothes on a rack. For them, there was no other place to hang a dream, a hope.

As I was meditating on the words etched on the base of the statue, I was reminded of Isaiah 61:1-3 and Luke 4:18-21—the ministry of Jesus.

Luke records that on one sabbath day, Jesus was in the synagogue to worship when He was handed the Book of Isaiah to read. He opened to chapter 61 and began to read the passage that prophesied His ministry. He closed the book, sat down, and said, "This day is this scripture fulfilled in your ears" (Luke 4:21). I don't think anyone listening that day understood what He really meant. As I began to study these verses, the Lord opened my understanding. Jesus said, that God, His Father, had anointed Him to preach good news to the meek. Why to the meek? Those who have a meek (humble) and gentle spirit will receive the things of God. Those who have the opposite kind of spirit will usually reject, argue, or defy the preaching of the Word.

Jesus was anointed to bind up the brokenhearted. Brokenhearted people will listen; they are looking for answers. They will receive any advice that will heal their broken, aching hearts.

Jesus was anointed to liberate the captives and open the prison to those who are bound. I do not believe this was necessarily in the physical—like jail—but in the spiritual and emotional realm. Captives are not merely in a prison or jail. Satan holds people captive by sickness, pain, and death. By lying to them, Satan makes them feel worthless in their mind, body, and spirit. When Satan gets us to believe his lies, we are, then, his captives.

Almost anyone who finds oneself in any of these circumstances will listen to one who has an answer. They will especially listen to one whose character is pure, whose heart is tender and compassionate, as was Jesus.

Those who are captives of the enemy will listen as they are looking for a way out of their captivity. They may not take the godly advice and use it to be set free, but at least they will listen.

Jesus was anointed to comfort those who mourn. Those who are grieving and mourning over the loss of a loved one will also listen to one who gives words of love, tenderness, and encouragement, or a hug that says, "I care."

Jesus was anointed to open the blinded eyes, both physical and spiritual. The unfortunate who are physi-

cally blind will also listen if they think there is a way
for them to see, whether by the laying on of hands,
anointing with oil and praying, or a new surgical tech-
nique.

It is no wonder Jesus said to the Pharisees, "They
that be whole need not a physician, but they that are
sick" (Matt. 9:12). The Pharisees were spiritually
blind. Jesus knew the needy would listen to Him and
receive from Him. He also knew those who thought
they had need of nothing would only ridicule, mock,
and reject Him. Yet those were the very ones Jesus
desperately wanted to reach as they, too, had need of
a Savior. If they only would have listened and received, their influence in the community would have
led many in the right direction. Those who thought
they had need of nothing were spiritual pygmies. In
their dire need they knew it not. Everyone is in need
of a Savior, for that is the greatest need of all.

Those who think of the *Statute of Liberty* as a savior
from their problems are often only looking at one
aspect—that is, physical prosperity or freedom. She
cannot promise prosperity to anyone, but she does lift
her lamp beside the golden door of opportunity and
freedom. Unlike Miss Liberty, Jesus our Savior lifts
His light toward the door of eternity and toward freedom from the bondage of Satan. Jesus says, "Come to
Me, all who are weary and heavy-laden, and I will give
you rest" (Matt. 11:28, NASB). Jesus says, "I am the
way, and the truth, and the life; no one comes to the
Father but through Me" (John 14:6, NASB). He is the

golden door to eternal life and He is living and real. He is not a symbol—He is reality.

Do you need to be free? Jesus said, "If the Son therefore shall make you free, ye shall be free indeed" (John 8:36).

Jesus is freedom! Jesus is liberty!

14

My Graceful Grand

An exquisite white grand piano with its matching bench dominates and graces our living room. It brings joy to the listener's ears as well as those who play at its keyboard. It is a gift from God. Let me start at the beginning and tell you how it came into my possession.

Music has been a part of my life since I was a little tot. My whole family is musically inclined. Music is as much a part of me as eating or sleeping.

As a child I would hear my mother plinking out a tune on the piano and I would come running, climb upon her lap, push her hands away, and pretend to play.

The year I began school, I also began piano lessons. I enjoyed learning on my own time but not on mother's scheduled time for me. Almost daily a malady crept over me that creeps over 99 percent of the music students; it's called laziness. The spirit of laziness could turn my sunny disposition into ugliness in a flash, and there it would linger until practice time was over. Ah, sweet escape from my mental metronome, preferably high in our apricot tree. No one looks for you there.

Music lessons were year round for seven years. My talent was God-given and needed to be fine tuned and yet I resisted. Unknowingly my stubbornness and rebellion crippled my talent for many years. Sin always does that to us.

After Jim and I were married, I longed for my piano; a vital part of me was missing. My parents shipped my ancient treasure to our home. I was delighted and would sit and play for hours. Somehow, I could always express the depth of my inner being at the keyboard. Every range of emotion is expressed in music.

Jim wasn't very excited at the looks of my archaic treasure and suggested we give it a coat of antiquing paint. Oh, horrors! It looked worse when we finished than it did before we started. Finally, we sold it, and a little part of my childhood left, too.

For a surprise, Jim took me to a piano store to pick out a new one. It didn't possess the tone quality of my old one, and truly I would rather have had a grand, but I dared not ask. My deepest desire from childhood was to own a grand piano, but I never thought it was possible, since they are very costly.

I played the new one, and all our children took piano lessons and practiced on it. During our move from a humid climate to a dry one, the wooden sounding board cracked. Never again would it hold a correct pitch.

I was convinced our youngest child, Joe, would be tone deaf while practicing every day if we didn't get a new piano. What should we do? Pianos are expensive. We hadn't priced one for fifteen years and never a grand. It's a good thing, too, or I wouldn't have had the courage to pray for one.

As I was pondering the situation, the Lord popped a Scripture into my heart, James 4:2, last part, and it solved the problem. "You do not have because you do not ask" (NASB).

"Oh, fool," I said aloud to myself, "how could you have missed it for over thirty-five years? You know God said He'd give you the desire of your heart if you delight yourself in Him" (see Ps. 37:4). I knew the verse well, but I'd never considered putting a grand piano in that category, even though I know He owns the cattle on a thousand hills. Since I knew God wasn't broke and on welfare, I asked Him for my heart's desire. I rarely generalize my prayers—instead I'm very specific. You receive what you ask for, so be very specific.

"Lord God," I prayed, "you know how long I've wanted a grand piano. Not for selfish reasons, Lord, but so I can praise you with my music and so Joe will not be tone deaf practicing on our broken piano. I'd like a white grand piano, please, with a matching bench. If you don't have a white one in your storehouse, then send a natural wood color, but, please, Lord, if black is all you have, don't send it. I don't want a black piano. Thank you, Lord, my piano is on its way; it's as good as being here already, Amen."

When I finished praying I realized God had heard and had already answered me. The Bible says He answers before we call.

Well, since God was processing my order I was

impressed to put my faith into action. First, I moved the old, broken little piano out of the house and then rearranged the furniture to accommodate my new grand piano. I could already imagine it sitting there proudly on the green carpet and framed by a white wall.

Nearly every day as I passed by the vacant spot in my living room, I'd thank the Lord for my piano that had not yet arrived. Jesus said, "If you abide in Me, and My words abide in you, ask whatever you wish, and it shall be done for you" (John 15:7, NASB). My responsibility to this promise was to act in accordance with the fact that God's Word is true, so I kept thanking Him for my piano. Eighteen months later my white grand piano with a matching bench arrived at our front door. Talk about excited, I was beside myself with joy! God did have one in the right color in His storehouse.

Later, after the deliverymen had gone, I was left alone with my new gift. Sitting at the keyboard, my heart was so full of gratitude all I could do was weep.

My desire is to praise and worship the King of kings and the Lord of lords with the talent He gave me on the gift of love He gave me. Truly He has given me the desire of my heart.

> I will make the Lord my music. I will make His love the key which tunes my heart to Him and gives my life its harmony. Author Unknown

15

Perseverance — Squirrel-Style

Several years ago we purchased a new type of bird feeder. It was about twelve inches long and five inches square. Along the front was a twelve-by-three-inch horizontal opening, just large enough for the smaller birds. It was made of clear Plexiglas for maximum bird watching and had two suction cups fastened on the back for attaching to a window. We placed the feeder in the center of an eight-foot-wide window, hoping at last the squirrels couldn't get to the birdseed. Now we sat back to watch from our front-row seats.

Soon the birds came and enjoyed an undisturbed feast. It wasn't long, though, until a hungry squirrel appeared with its nose in the air. He smelled food but couldn't figure out how to reach it. Squirrels are smart, persistent, and sometimes destructive in their quest for food.

This one began to pace in front of the window. You could almost see the wheels of contemplation turning in its head. We soon saw his plan of attack. It was to climb the side of the house and leap to the bird feeder. After the first try he found himself back on the ground.

Climb, fall—climb, fall. He must have tried it for twenty minutes. Finally he caught the hang of it and jumped onto the siding, dug in his toenails and climbed vertically five feet. He hoped to leap wide enough to land on the feeder. Of course, he missed the target and ended up on the ground. He would not be deterred and kept up with an admirable persistence you rarely find in man or beast.

Our son, Jim, and I were spellbound with the intelligence and perseverance of this fluffy-tailed fur ball. It almost came to the point where we would cheer him on to help him reach his goal.

In utter fatigue and frustration the squirrel left his challenge and probably went home to contemplate the best plan of attack. Would it be a new plan or just plain old persistence?

Sure enough, the next morning Jim and I were waiting when he reappeared on the scene. He took one giant leap, and up the siding he climbed, leaped again toward the feeder, and fell. Squirrels are so agile they always land on their feet. Again we watched in amused amazement and laughed each time he fell.

Climb, leap, fall—climb, leap, fall—over and over again, always one target in sight, always one goal in mind. I watched while my housework patiently waited. This was too good to miss; it was better than the Olympics.

Nearly an hour passed before he finally reached his target. He was so big his furry tail hung out of the feeder. This feeder was declared "squirrel proof," and we really thought it was. This feat would be impossible for a squirrel. Don't underestimate one. From then on if the birds weren't in the feeder we could expect to find a big bushy tail hanging out of it.

I am reminded of the parable Jesus used to teach perseverance in prayer without becoming discouraged because of answers not arriving immediately.

> There was in a certain city a judge who did not fear God, and did not respect man. And there was a widow in that city, and she kept coming to him, saying, Give me legal protection from my opponent. And for a while he was unwilling; but afterward he said to himself, Even though I do not fear God nor respect man, yet because this widow bothers me, I will give her legal protection, lest by continually coming she wear me out (Luke 18:2-5, NASB).

I can assure you that you will never weary your Heavenly Father with your petitions. You can always keep coming; He is always there to listen and give you an answer. Just remember His answers are on His timetable, not ours. He is faithful and will bring about the answers to His children's requests. Sometimes His answers are "yes," sometimes they are "no," and often they are "wait."

For example, we may request of God salvation for a child. Claim a Bible verse for that child like Isaiah 49:25 (last part) or Psalm 138:8, then thank God for bringing that lost one to Him. This is where our persistence comes in. Continuously thank God that His Word is true. His promises are faithful, and we can expect Him to bring about circumstances so this child will receive salvation.

My persistence isn't going to change God's mind one bit. He had salvation in mind for the child when Jesus died on the cross. My persistence is in thanking Him for the salvation He has already provided and knowing my child will receive it. Continuously thanking Him for what He's doing helps me not to despair while the answer is coming. I can focus on the solution and not the problem. It helps me to remember the words of Jesus, "[Men] ought to pray and not to lose heart" (Luke 18:1, NASB).

Keep on praying, keep on thanking Him. The answer is on the way.

16

Hit by a Truck

My husband, Jim, and I had just arrived in Malacca, Malaysia, after two gloriously blessed weeks of ministry in Australia.

It was time for Jim to check with his office back home to see if anything of importance needed his attention.

He was told the shocking news that our twenty-year-old daughter, Jan, had been hit by a truck while riding her bicycle. My heart said, "No, not again!" Four years earlier, to the month, when Jim and I were ministering in Norway, we had a similar phone call. Jan had been hit by a car as she sat on our front porch. She had nearly lost her leg. Why was she being tortured and tormented again? My body went numb, but my mind hit the overdrive button.

It was Jan's first minitriathlon competition. A minitriathlon consists of three events, swimming one-half mile, running three miles, and bicycling fifteen miles. The three events are endured consecutively. Jan wanted so much to complete all the events successfully to prove to the doctors and her friends that Jesus truly had healed her leg from the car accident.

She had consulted an orthopedic surgeon a week before the race, and he advised her not to compete in the running—the pounding wouldn't be good for her leg. She was only more determined than ever to compete and finish the race. She had been healed. We knew it, too, for we had been witnesses to her healing.

Jan had almost finished the race. She could see the finish line a mile and a half away as she pedaled furiously. She was high on excitement and, oh, so happy.

Suddenly, out of nowhere, a truck appeared and made a left turn at the same time Jan arrived at the intersection. She was hit broadside by the truck. She screamed as she and her bicycle flew through the air and landed on the pavement with a thud. Both skidded and stopped under the wheels of another truck which had stopped at the intersection.

Jan was fortunate that she had worn her biking helmet. The helmet was cracked, but her head and brain were protected from injury. God had spared her life!

Within ten seconds an orthopedic surgeon was at her side. He, too, was in the race, but his bicycle had broken down and he had been forced to push it. Had he been riding instead, he would have already crossed the finish line. Don't tell me God doesn't order the steps of a righteous man or woman!

As we related these events to a dear, godly pastor in Malaysia, he stopped where he was walking (in the middle of the street) and said, "Let's pray."

The Spirit of God came upon him as he claimed

Psalm 34:19-20 for Jan. "Many are the afflictions of the righteous: but the Lord delivereth him out of them all. He keepeth all his bones; not one of them is broken" We agreed with him as he prayed that the bone be healed in Jesus' name. He thanked God for doing it, then looked at his watch, and said, "It's three o'clock, PM." We made a mental note of the time. We believed and knew God had healed our Jan again. In just six days we'd know all the details when we arrived in California.

We walked into the hotel where Jan worked at the front desk. Sure enough, she was there, working. Yes, she was healed, but she was still bruised and sore. Yes, at the time the pastor had claimed healing for Jan she was resting and sleeping soundly for the first time since the accident. Praise the Holy Name of Jesus, He is still our Healer today!

The accident had given Jan severe pavement burns, many bruises, and a broken collar bone. That's all. Five weeks after her accident, Jan entered another mini-triathlon and finished.

She had wanted only one testimony to God's healing power in her body. Instead, He gave her two. Isn't God good?

17

Streams of Living Waters

A wealthy rancher had many acres where he grazed his cattle. In the midst ran a bubbly, singing brook. The animals would slake their thirst in its refreshing waters.

One summer a tiny, frail sapling of a tree was planted close to the bank of the stream. It didn't take long for the roots to reach the life-giving flow beneath the tree. Nourished at the stream's breast, the sapling quickly grew into a mammoth tree. The cattle rested in its shade, birds built nests and cradled their young in its leafy boughs; little children played in its shadow and climbed its limbs. A beautiful sight was this magnificent handiwork of God.

Then one day the rancher decided the stream would be of more benefit if it flowed directly by his house. So with great earthmoving machines a new channel was gouged in the ground, and the surging water was diverted into its new course. The old stream lay barren. The rocks which once glistened, as the sun reflected its bright face in the water that flowed over them, now stood stark and desolate. Worst of all, the lush grass withered and the lovely green tree drooped. Without the life-sustaining flow, the tree grimly struggled to survive: The next summer its leaves did not burst forth, and the tree died.

The rancher may not have considered such consequences, or perhaps he did but was willing to pay the price.

I believe we as Christians have the same cost to consider.

God who made the heavens and earth, who carved the rivers and streams with His fingers, who ordered the seasons and planted the flowers, grass, and all growing things, who set the birds, the cattle, and all living creatures on the face of His creation knows the principle forgotten by man. The principle is found in Psalm 1:1-3. "Blessed is the man that walketh not in the counsel of the ungodly, nor standeth in the way of sinners, nor sitteth in the seat of the scornful" (v. 1).

God says, Don't *walk* with, *sit* with, or *stand* with the godless lest their behavior rub off on you. "But his delight is in the law of the Lord; and in His law does he meditate day and night" (v. 2).

In other words, don't spend your time with those who don't love the Lord; instead feed on the Word of God and meditate on it day and night. Meditate means to chew on it like a cow does her cud. She chews, swallows and digests from the first stomach, then starts all over again into the second stomach, chewing, swallowing, and digesting. She makes the most of her eating, chewing, and digesting.

The Bible says if we do the first and second verses,

the third one shall be our reward. "And he shall be like a tree planted by the rivers of water, that brings forth his fruit in his season; his leaf shall not wither; and whatsoever he doeth shall prosper" (v. 3).

Friend, if we want to prosper and grow in the Lord we must obey these Scriptures. They are as valid today as the day they were written.

The newly planted baby believer who drinks daily from the pure stream of God's Word is nourished and eventually grows into a spiritual giant. Take away or neglect the nourishment, however, and the spirit withers, and the heart becomes dry and barren.

Oh, foolish Christians, we who choose decay instead of vitality while neglecting the food God has provided for our daily sustenance—His blessed Word.

Christians, let us be the ones to prosper at the hand of God. It is our reward for obedience in living a godly life and delighting to study and meditate on the Word of God.

We serve a good, gracious, and generous God. Oh, taste and see that the Lord is good. Experience His faithfulness.

Let us feed upon His Word daily. Let us become that tree planted by the river of waters, and let us bring forth our fruit in due season.

18

The Champion

Gentle Ben? Well, I guess you could call him that, but actually he was Joy's pet rat. A rat was required for a project in her high school psychology class. The topic was behavior modification. A boy at school had built a large wire-mesh cage for a rat. It was a 36-inch-square cube with several series of ladders with platforms attached. There was also a small (4″ X 4″) platform in the center that was made like a swing.

Joy's object was to train Ben to climb the first ladder and find the reward, a nut, she had placed on the first platform. Second, he was to climb a little higher, on ladder number two, to the second platform where he would find another almond. From the second platform, she hoped to teach him how to reach the little swing which also held a nut. The only way to the swing was by pulling the wires toward him until the swing was moving much like a trapeze. His timing was crucial. If he was off just a fraction of a second, he'd fall to the bottom of the cage. While perched precariously on the swing, he had one more challenge to master before he was a champion. While the little platform was swinging, he must scamper to one more higher platform on the side of the cage which held his last reward.

After Joy explained all this to me, I looked at the cage, then at furry little Ben, then at Joy, and back to the cage. *Oh, my,* I thought as I shook my head in wonder. "Do you really think you can teach that little fellow how to do all these tricks?" I asked. "Of course, I can," was her confident reply. It surely looked impossible to me. Ben was small and skinny looking, and I had misgivings that he could ever do requirement number three, the swinging platform.

Joy knew exactly what her plan would be. It would take time, but modifying behavior always does. When he was ready to learn something new, she would withhold food all that day. At evening when she placed him in his training center, he would catch the scent of food and hustle right up the ladder to the platform to eat. She continued the same routine until the trick was no longer a challenge. I watched in amazement.

Week after week Ben mastered new accomplishments. Joy also spent valuable time holding, stroking, feeding, loving, and talking to him. It wasn't long until he grew fat from overeating. Unfortunately for him, it was about the same time to learn the difficult trick. Could he get the platform to swing and climb aboard without always ending up on the bottom of the cage? I watched; he fell. He fell again. He never gave up; I was proud of him. For a couple of nuts or a pinch of cheese, Ben would persist and do almost any impossible trick. I was totally convinced Joy could teach him to do anything. He finally mastered the quick timing, and it was nothing for him to climb from the swing while it was in motion and land on the last platform. By the time he finished learning all his tricks, he had grown very long and very fat. He didn't fit into his swing anymore and hung over on all sides.

It had been a fun and fascinating experience for me to watch how food could become a catalyst to behavior modification in an animal. Could this procedure also apply to people? Probably. This approach could apply not only physically but mentally and spiritually, too.

Jesus said, "Blessed are they which do hunger and thirst after righteousness: for they shall be filled" (Matt. 5:6). When we hunger after the things of God and go to the Source to be filled, we learn we can change mentally and spiritually. Yes, with daily meditation in God's Word we shall not be conformed to this world, but we shall be transformed by renewing our minds (Rom. 12:2). Transformed from carnal, worldly thoughts and acts to thoughts and acts of God.

The food of the Word of God will change our attitudes and behavior. The change is from the realm of the flesh into a one-spirit union with God. Truly, we shall be filled with the Spirit just like Jesus promised when we hunger and thirst after the right standing with God.

19

Surprise

Nearly thirteen years have passed since the day I received a very special package in the mail.

The return address was unfamiliar, as was the handwriting, but it was clearly addressed to Mrs. James Irwin.

I had not ordered anything by mail. It was not my birthday. *Whatever could be in the package?* I thought. Excitedly, I yanked off the string and tore at the brown wrapping paper. I carefully saved the return address in the upper left-hand corner.

Enclosed was a letter written in very shaky penmanship. It began:

Dear Mrs. Irwin,

Since it is my birthday I would like to send you a gift. Our Lord said it is more blessed to give than to receive. For my birthday I am sending you this five-pound bag of shelled pecans.

Signed

For a moment I was speechless. How unusual, a total stranger chose to give me a gift. Did she know, had she learned something I had not learned? No, I also knew the same verse of Scripture but had never dreamed of practicing it in that way. But why not?

The apostle Paul in the Book of Acts reiterates the words of Jesus. ". . . remember the words of the Lord Jesus, how he said, It is more blessed to give than to receive" (20:35).

In the Gospel of Luke, Jesus also told us how to give. "Give, and it will be given to you; good measure, pressed down, shaken together, running over, they will pour into your lap. For by your standard of measure it will be measured to you in return" (Luke 6:38, NASB).

"The imagery is of a container of grain filled to the brim with grain and running over the edge. Our liberality should be like that" (*Ryrie Study Bible*, p. 1450).

The package was still in my thoughts a few weeks later as my birthday rolled around. I wanted to give something to someone for my birthday. Instead of someone, I gave to a group. I was in turn blessed beyond measure. That sweet little old lady's idea was like the ripples in a pond after tossing in a pebble.

God's word is so true. My heart was truly running over with joy after I had given. That was my reward.

20

Imprinting

Feller was the name my mother gave a wild baby duck my brother Claire and I found. It was tiny, fragile, and afraid when we first saw it swimming alone in a pond at the city park. It was crying loudly for its mother. There were no other ducks to be seen in that area of the park so we couldn't figure out how that lonely little fellow came to be in a big pond by himself.

With compassion in our youthful hearts, we decided Claire should wade in after it, and we would take it home and be its mother. As my brother waded toward the little orphan, it cried louder and paddled frantically until Claire caught it in his small hands. Holding it closely to him, he headed toward the bank. We dried the frightened duckling with our blanket and cuddled it for warmth.

It wasn't long until Dad and Mother decided it was time to leave the park and go home. We held Feller gently all the way home. He was very cozy, comforted, and sleeping quietly.

It was a joy to have such an unusual pet in our fenced

backyard. He seemed happy, too, exploring his new surroundings.

Week after week we watched him grow strong on chicken feed and wondered when this brown duck was going to get its glorious male colors. Surprise! He was a she, and she wasn't going to have glorious male colors.

One of her favorite pastimes was going to the vegetable garden with us while we weeded. She usually stayed close by. Sometimes she would be absorbed in tracking down a bug and wouldn't see us move from her range of sight. Upon missing us, she would peep loudly and stretch her neck, looking over the plants for us. As soon as we called her she would quickly waddle her way to our sides, peeping loudly all the way.

In the fall Mother said it was time to take her back to her birthplace. She had matured, and it was where she belonged. It was the right thing to do we knew, but we still wanted to keep her. She had been so loving and gave us so much joy.

We took her back to the large duck pond but were soon saddened. The other ducks did not accept her. Instead they pecked at her with their bills, making her feel unwelcome. She didn't understand. After all she looked like them, she acted like them, and they all spoke the same language; but this newcomer was an outsider.

As we turned to leave, she caught sight of us and hurriedly came out of the water. She shook her wet feathers, waddled after us, and we all went home.

Puzzled about the other ducks' behavior toward

Feller, and just what to do, had Claire and me stumped. We asked Mother. She suggested we get the big, old, galvanized washtub from the garage and fill it with water. "She'll learn to dive and live in the water just like the other ducks; then in two weeks we'll try to leave her again and she'll probably stay." It was a wise decision. Mother was right. Feller loved the water and dunked her head a lot.

In two weeks we took her back to the pond. This time as she swam away she was self-confident, and the others must have sensed it. She was accepted. We watched her for a while to make sure the others wouldn't torment her, then turned to leave with a bittersweet emptiness in our hearts and tears in our eyes. She didn't follow. It had been so much fun to be her surrogate mothers. Feller had really been accepted at last.

Each time we came to the park to feed the ducks we would call her name. Although she never ran to us again, we knew which one she was since she had the habit of looking up when a plane flew overhead. None of the other ducks did this.

Some thirty-five years later I took a psychology course in college and found that this experience I had with a wild baby duck was similar to what an Australian scientist, Lorenz, had experienced in 1935. The following was his experiment.

"A set of eggs laid by a goose was divided into two groups. One-half of the eggs were hatched by the mother goose, who thus became the first living thing the goose-hatched goslings saw. Predictable, they followed her around and kept close to her. But the other half of the eggs were hatched in an incubator, and a scientist was the first living thing the goslings saw. The goslings reacted to the scientist in the same way the other goslings had reacted to their mother. They followed the scientist and kept close to him."[1]

This God-given phenomenon is called "imprinting." Scientists say that rarely, if ever, do birds who have been imprinted follow another "mother."

How exciting it was for me to recognize that God had given us children "an-exception-to-the-rule experience" with Feller. But then I serve an exceptional God. Don't you?

As I thought about the word *imprinting,* I was reminded of the two blind men in Matthew 20:29-34, who were sitting beside the dusty, narrow road that led out of Jericho. A great multitude of people was also on that road following Jesus, asking Him questions and talking among themselves.

I can almost hear the blind men's conversation as they heard the approaching commotion. "What's causing all this stir among our people? I wonder who is visiting our town." As they listened they heard the name of Jesus mentioned. Is it? Could it be? They were familiar with His name, for His fame had gone out far and wide. They also knew He was the healer.

"[Jesus]," they hollered. "Have mercy on us." Some of the crowd closest to the blind men told them to be still. They said Jesus had no time for the likes of them, the outcasts. "Don't bother the Master; He is busy teaching." The blind men would not be intimidated and hollered all the louder. "Have mercy on us, thou Son of David" (v. 31).

Jesus heard them and stopped. When Jesus stopped, everyone stopped. He drew close to the two men. All attention was focused on these ragged, dirty blind men. He looked down on them with deep compassion and asked, "What do you want Me to do for you?" They pleadingly answered, "Lord, we want our eyes to be opened" (vv. 32-33, NASB).

Our loving Lord bent close and touched their blind eyes. Instantly, they could see. Their eyesight forever framed a portrait of their Healer, Jesus, and the Bible says they followed Him. They had been "imprinted" for life by the Savior.

When our spiritually blind eyes are opened, will we, too, follow Him? If you have been imprinted by the world instead of Jesus, it is possible to be reimprinted just like our little wild duck. You can choose whom you will follow. "But as for me and my house, we will serve the Lord" (Josh. 24:15).

21

An Unmerited Gift

Our recent trip to Australia produced many blessings for us. The most blessed events were watching God change lives.

Upon arriving in Melbourne, we were whisked off to Ansett Airlines' executive dining room. There was a small luncheon planned for six. That's where I met Mary.

She was mayoress of a small township within Melbourne. "A happy extrovert" is the how I would describe her. She was about my age, and I liked her immediately. We chatted all through the meal. The more I learned about her the more I felt we were very much alike. She was not a stranger to me.

After lunch we were to be escorted to our hotel for a few hours of much-needed rest. The meeting the night before had kept us up until past midnight, and we had a very early morning departure. I already had visions of a deliciously long sleep before the evening meeting. Instead of a nap, God had other plans for me.

Mary turned to me and said, "Since I'm the mayoress I have the use of a chauffeured limousine. It is parked just outside and, if you like, I'll be happy to show you the city or take you shopping."

Sightseeing was the last thing I would have chosen to do that day, but down deep in my spirit I knew that was not the real reason she wanted me to go. "Sure, let's go," was my reply. God had ordained this meeting, and I wasn't going to miss what He was doing. We drove around nearly forty-five minutes, then headed toward her home.

Mary gave me a quick "Cook's Tour" of her home and offered to make me a cup of herb tea. She suggested I relax for awhile as she set the water on to boil. I joined her in the kitchen, and we continued with our conversation. She picked up her knitting from the table and worked quickly with flashing needles.

On my tour of the house, I had spotted a lovely grand piano in her living room. I had a longing to sit and play for awhile and asked if I might. I miss playing mine when we are on the road. She invited me to sit and play as long as I wished while she made the tea.

I marveled at how at home I felt. I had just met this woman three hours earlier, and yet there was something which seemed to unite our hearts like old friends. I couldn't identify the feeling.

In ten minutes Mary appeared, carrying two steaming cups of Red Zinger tea and her knitting. We continued to share many things. I told her how, through God's Word and the prayer of faith, I had received my grand piano. Mostly, she seemed hungry for the Word of God so I gave it to her. She went to church, but it was a dead church. She didn't know a personal Jesus. I shared mine. He is my best friend.

As we talked, she finished her knitting project. It was one of the most beautiful sweaters I had ever seen. It was lovingly and creatively knitted in shades of vibrant aqua, medium blue, and light gray, with loosely woven silver threads in the long sleeves. The finishing touch was three tiny silver lamé bows on the left front. It was her original creation, one of a kind. Holding it up, she handed it to me and said, "It's for you." I nearly choked on the hot tea as I felt a cry coming on. It was the second time in my life I had been so touched that I almost burst into tears over a stranger's unmerited gift to me. She had not created it for me; how could I take it?

Mary insisted as she spoke softly, "You, my friend, are so very much like me." Ah, she had sensed it, too; it wasn't my imagination. She had called me "friend." A stranger had never said that to me before. She continued, "I make these sweaters for and give them to my friends."

I accepted her gift of love and friendship. The sweater makes me feel very special when I wear it.

All too soon, the afternoon was over, and it was time to return to the hotel and prepare for the evening meeting. Had God ordered my day? Oh, yes. If I had gone to the hotel immediately after lunch, I would surely have missed a special blessing He had planned for me.

Looking back on this unique event, I am reminded of another event that took place nearly two thousand years ago. It was the most unique event ever on planet Earth.

Jesus had willingly gone to the cross, in love, for me. The ultimate sacrifice of His life was given so I would have everlasting life *if* I would receive His gift.

Eternal life, like my sweater, was not earned, asked for, or merited in any way. It was a gift of love from the Father. It was finished and offered to me. I could take it or leave it. I could receive it or reject it. I chose to receive the gift of eternal life by believing in Jesus as the Son of God. John 3:36 says, "He who believes in the Son has eternal life" (NASB).

In his Letter to the Ephesians, Paul writes, "For by grace you have been saved through faith; and that not of yourselves, it is the gift of God; not as a result of works, that no one should boast" (Eph. 2:8-9, NASB).

I enjoy my beautiful sweater very much, but nothing will ever compare or compete with the greatest gift of all—the gift of living forever with my King, my Lord and my God.

22

Sitting at His Feet

As a small child, I clearly remember certain occasions when I would be with my mother away from our house. Those times we spent shopping in the big department stores or stopping at the corner drugstore for a root beer float. They were rare occurrences, I admit. That's why they are remembered.

Sometimes I would become fatigued or bored and long to sit down, especially in a busy doctor's office with all the chairs filled. Then Mother would do something special for me. While sitting in her chair, she would place both feet close together and tilt the back of her heels upward. That made a lovely, warm, and fairly comfortable place for a child to sit for as long as necessary. She also made this little "footstool" for me every morning when she brushed and finger-curled my hair. It was a special place for me to sit.

My youngest brother and I would sit at Mother's feet for hours on the Lord's Day listening to her read Bible stories. Unknowingly, I was not only sitting at Mother's feet listening, but she was also leading me to the feet of Jesus where one day that would be the one and only desire of my heart.

Long, long ago she told me the name of her favorite song, "Sitting at the Feet of Jesus." As a child I never really understood why it was her favorite. Thirty years later I understood. Sitting at His feet is where she learned to trust Him.

In the New Testament, "at Jesus' feet" seems to be a special place. At His feet we see individuals giving adoration, thanksgiving, love, humility, and a listening ear to His words. I can't decide which story is my favorite. We often hear Mary and Martha's story where Mary spent her time at the feet of Jesus. Instead of studying their story, let's turn in the Gospel of Luke to chapter 8, verses 26-39, and look at the story of the demoniac. You know this story well, too.

Jesus and His disciples had just sailed across the Sea of Galilee to the country of the Gerasenes. They climbed out of the boat and pulled it upon the sandy shore. Turning around, they were startled to see a man standing there who was stark naked and muttering to himself. Their eyes focused on his filthy, dirt-caked body, splattered with self-inflicted wounds that were infected. His hair was long, dirty, matted, and wild-looking. His eyes had the same appearance as his hair —wild and tormented. This pitiful-looking man was so full of demons he was insane and lived in the grave-yard among the tombs. He was usually shackled and chained like an animal. The demons in him were so strong that the man possessed supernatural strength and kept breaking his fetters so he could roam freely.

I visualize him as a wild-eyed, wild-haired Charles Manson—only worse. His appearance must have terrorized the villagers.

It also must have unnerved and made silent the disciples as they looked at him. Remember, they had just crossed the Sea of Galilee in a violent storm and thought they were going to die. I doubt that their nerves had settled down from that experience, and here was another storm facing them in the flesh.

As the demoniac stood before Jesus, the demons recognized Him as the Son of God. The man fell to his face and worshiped at Jesus' feet. Then, rising to his knees, he cried out, "What have I to do with you, Jesus, Son of the Most High God? I beg You, do not torment me" (v. 27, NASB). Jesus spoke softly and tenderly to the man, "[Son,] What is your name?" The demoniac replied, "Legion" (v. 30). In a firm voice, Jesus commanded the demons to leave this man. They spoke to Him, requesting permission to enter into a herd of pigs feeding nearby. Permission was granted. The legion of demons left the man and entered the pigs. (A Roman legion contained 3,000-6,000 foot soldiers.) The now demon-possessed pigs ran wildly toward the lake and into the water and drowned. This was shocking behavior for pigs to all who were watching.

The next scene that appears in Scripture is tranquillity. Jesus, appearing on the scene, always brings tranquillity. The news of the delivered demoniac spread instantly like a wild, windswept fire. People poured out of their dwellings to come and see this man who, only moments before, had been a wild-eyed, raving maniac. There he was, a vision of peace, with clothes on, and in his right mind, sitting at the feet of Jesus.

The Bible does not tell us how long he sat there, fifteen minutes or an hour. I can almost feel the instant bonding. He would not be separated from his Deliverer. Later, as Jesus and the disciples were getting into their boat to depart, the man begged Jesus to "Please, let me go with you." Jesus said, "No, I have other plans for you. You go to your home and tell everyone you know and meet what God has done for you" (vv. 38-39, author's words). The man was to be a witness for Jesus.

Beloved, it is the same for us today as it was two thousand years ago. We are never the same after we meet Jesus. His appearance in our lives always brings tranquillity and an instant bonding. I can't explain why. I only know it does. When we meet our Deliverer, our Savior, face to face, we always want to sit at His feet. We desire to sit there to be taught by Him and to be loved by Him.

Will you come with me today to worship at His feet and adore Him? He is worthy of our adoration, praise, and worship. He is our Deliverer.

23

Rotten Pears

Hot August days and the cool nights of September —ah, canning season had abruptly appeared on schedule once again. I found myself stationed in the kitchen, laboriously peeling and coring bushels of pears. Waiting patiently nearby were dozens of clean, empty fruit jars. I sensed a long day ahead of me.

The pears were unusually colorful this year. They looked like some tiny little elf had been busily dabbing earth tones of radiant color over the cheeks of each fruit. Turning one carefully over in my hand, I was amazed at the consistency of glorious color and the firmness of its flesh. The peelings slipped off easily, exposing a white interior. Then, using a sharp paring knife, I sliced it from top to bottom.

What a shocking revelation! At the very center, the core was mushy, soft, and rotting. Disappointment crept over me as I looked at the situation. How in the world could a beautiful, fresh fruit have a rotten heart? Were there any more like it? Yes, I found out later, there were many.

My mind began to reflect on Scripture. Somewhere

it dealt with that very problem with people. What a parallel. There are times when we may appear to others by our actions, words, or our manner of dress that everything is just fine with us; all the while allowing them to believe untruths about our spiritual and emotional conditions and never dealing with the mushy rottenness of our own hearts.

God spoke to the prophet-judge Samuel concerning the one He was going to anoint king over Israel.

> Do not look at his appearance or at the height of his stature, because I have rejected him; *for God sees not as man sees, for man looks at the outward appearance, but the Lord looks at the heart"* (1 Sam. 16:7, NASB, author's italics).

The prophet Jeremiah seems to drive home at the root of the problem. "The heart is more deceitful than all else And is desperately sick; who can understand it? I, the Lord, search the heart, I test the mind" (Jer. 17:9-10, NASB).

Beloved, we do not need to be kept in bondage to our inner self. We can be free of sinful attitudes, thoughts, and behavior as we come to Jesus. Jesus came to set the captives free. Cry out with a repentant heart just like the publican did in the parable in Luke 18:12-14.

That publican felt so unworthy he could not lift his eyes toward heaven. He beat upon his breast while crying out to the Father, "God, be merciful to me a sinner" (v. 13). He went home a forgiven man. Today you can, too.

24

Drouth

Jim was preparing to leave for an extended trip overseas. Before leaving he decided to do some planting. He had bought a dynamic kit on raising vegetables in the house. He planted some very tiny seeds in miniature peat moss pots. He fed and watered them carefully, with visions of a ready-to-eat crop upon his return.

He left his eighty-six year old mother (who was living with us) instructions on how to water, feed, and care for them, then hastily left on his trip.

Within two weeks many of the seeds had sprouted, and others were doing their best to come up under less-than-ideal conditions. I watched Jim's project with interest as mold began to appear on top of some of the little peat moss pots. Mold means sure death unless drastic measures are taken to reverse the process. The plants were sitting in a window with almost no sun. They needed a lot of sun to keep the pots, seeds, and plants warm.

It wasn't long before Mom forgot to water them, so occasionally I would help with a little sprinkling. By and by the little plants began to experience drouth.

It is difficult for me to watch a plant die without nursing it to health. I have many houseplants to care for and keep healthy. However, I saw an opportunity for the family to learn a most valuable lesson. I left Jim's tiny plants alone. Very shortly, they all succumbed for lack of care or concern.

When Jim returned and saw his dead plants, his face drooped with disappointment. "What happened?" he questioned. I lovingly suggested maybe he should wait until he was home for an extended period before planting again, so he could care for his seedlings.

You see, planting a seed is like beginning a relationship. Before that relationship can flourish, it needs gentle nurturing, watering, love, care, and warmth of the Son.

This same thing can happen to new baby Christians, as well as older ones in the faith. Our relationship with Jesus depends upon us, not Him. He's always there, ready to listen, guide, love, and speak to your heart if you will only listen.

The enemy would like for us not to water and care for our relationship with Jesus. He would like for you to neglect the renewing of your mind daily in the Word of God (Rom. 12:2). Satan wants you to let the darkness and dampness of this world grow the mold of spiritual death and decay. He doesn't want you to be in the Sonshine. The Bible says he wants to rip you off (John 10:10). He wants to steal away your time with God through your Bible study and prayer time. He'll also keep you away from church and other Christians, too, if he can. Once he can get you isolated, he'll try to damage your relationship with Jesus.

Take care, dear one, to nuture carefully your relationship with Jesus. Water it; care for it.

A. Daily Bible study—study even it it's only ten minutes

B. Prayer—all through the day talk to Jesus like He was your closest friend.

C. Confession—keep short accounts of sin; confess immediately.

D. Listen—train the ears of your spirit to listen to the Spirit of God.

E. Share Jesus—give a word of testimony about what Jesus means to you.

Now, walk with God and enjoy the greatest of all relationships this world has ever known. For surely we are the trees of righteousness, planted by the Lord that He might be glorified (see Isa. 61:3).

25

Master Refinisher

A small flyer was lying on top of the check-out counter of a tiny restaurant. My eyes wandered to the small black print on the pale aqua paper. It read, "Yearly antique sale." Beneath the advertisement a phone number was given, also a woman's name.

Normally I pay no attention to antiques of any kind. Today was different. I had been looking for a few select pieces to furnish my wee, cozy cabin on the hill behind our home. The comfort of my special hideaway was important to me. Sometimes I would sit in the cabin daydreaming about what piece of furniture would look perfect in a certain place.

What I knew about antiques you could write on the head of a pin. I just knew I wanted some old, comfortable looking and feeling furniture at a low price.

Upon arriving at home, I picked up the telephone and dialed the number printed on the paper. A woman answered and assured me the prices of her furniture were lower, by half, than all the shops in Colorado Springs. The shipment of seven hundred pieces was due from England in two weeks. She promised to call

me the moment they arrived, and I could come and
have a look at them. I dreamed on.

The big day arrived. With detailed directions to her
house in hand, I set out for the countryside. Arriving
at her home I saw furniture everywhere—inside and
outside. Many people were milling around searching
for just the right treasure to call their own. Many were
hauling pieces away as fast as the lady could take their
money. I thought to myself, *The way they are grabbing
this furniture, this truly must be a bargain.* I am not one
to pass up a good bargain. I stood around rather wide-
eyed at the whole scenerio. Was I about to be caught
in a new trap called a hobby or embarking on a venture
called "antique collecting"? I hoped not, and I knew
for sure my unsuspecting husband hoped not. I joined
the teeming mass, anyway.

Looking carefully, I mentally selected each piece. I
wanted only oak. It was difficult for me to distinguish
the type of wood since it had a dark old stain with
layers of shellac or varnish covering it. As I stood
contemplating a piece, I could envision the work that
loomed ahead. Thinking about the caustic, smelly
paint and varnish remover, gooey shellac being lifted
off the furniture, and the untold hours of sanding,
nearly talked me into going home and forgetting I had
ever seen the flyer.

Summoning up my courage, I selected dining room
chairs and a small side cupboard. Obviously, I was
committed. After paying my bill I headed homeward
with all my old treasures. Then I remembered the piles
of nasty, dirty, old rags, mountains of gummy and

frayed steel wool pads, and reams of sandpaper that always accompany such a project. At a moment like this a person just might question their sanity. I would be courageous and see the challenge through.

A few days later I had pumped up my courage to tackle the first chair. I dragged it and all the accompanying paraphernalia for refinishing furniture outside. First, I applied that caustic, smelly varnish remover, then waited until either the varnish became crinkly or my rubber gloves got eaten through with holes. Next, I began to remove the whole mushy mess with steel wool pads. The first attempt looked so hopeless and disappointing, I was ready to trash it all; and the smeary disorder was simply undefinable. Take heart, under all that disfiguration was a tiny glimmer of what the whole would look like after complete stripping. The grain of the wood was beautifully exposed, light in color, and magnificent with character. Seeing it that way gave me courage to go on with the job, even though I knew the sanding process seemed like an eternity.

Sanding the chair took two days. It was restored to its original light color, and it was beautiful. With the sanding finished, the miracle worker called tung oil was applied. That wonderful special oil soaked into the newly sanded surface and gave the furniture a golden glow. It was warm to the touch and thoroughly beautiful with the grain enhanced. I took a step back to admire the marvelous transformation that had just taken place. A little polishing with a soft cloth, and the job was finished.

That lovely refinished chair reminds me of someone I know. I was acquainted with her before she met the Master Refinisher, and I know her now. What a change! What a difference!

I'll call her Polly. Her life was darkly stained with sins of sexual immorality, excessive fears, cursing, drugs for sleeping, drugs for staying awake, drugs for depression and nervousness. She was under psychiatric care, and had been for many years, but to no avail. Polly's varnish came in the form of over thirty wigs. With a wig she could become anyone she wanted to be, except herself. She didn't know who she was and didn't like what she thought she was. She was nearly successful in committing suicide. I had not heard from her in nearly twenty-five years, and I'll never know why she placed a call to me two years ago. Her situation sounded hopeless as her drug-dulled mind cried out to me for help. My heart was breaking for her. I shared my loving Jesus with her. I told Polly that He was the only answer to her problems. He was the greatest psychiatrist that ever lived and the only one she needed. She was dubious but had nothing to lose in giving Jesus a try. Before she hung up the phone, we promised to keep in touch, and I prayed with her.

I vowed aloud to myself, *I will love her to Jesus and let Him change her.* Each time she called, I shared Jesus with her, told her I loved her, then prayed with her before we hung up. It wasn't long before I could sense a small change. Little by little, God applied the varnish remover. Layer after layer came off. Drug after drug wasn't needed anymore. One day Jesus got to bare wood. She called, ecstatic with joy, and reported she had just given away all her wigs. She didn't need them anymore. As a matter of fact she was rather liking herself a bit, and those she worked with were liking her a whole lot more. There was excitement in her voice that hadn't been there previously. All I could do was praise God.

The next call, I knew she was off of all drugs. Her voice was happy, giggly, and clear. Polly had met Jesus and no longer needed to see the psychiatrist. I cried with joy.

The grain of her character was being sanded, and the real person shone through. She was becoming radiant. Several months later, a new Polly was reborn, and she followed her Lord in water baptism. He had been sanding her with fine grit and was ready to apply the oil of His Holy Spirit upon her. It would bring out her true inner beauty with a warm glow. It was difficult to believe this was the same person who had called me ten months earlier in the depths of living hell and despair.

Only the Master Refinisher can strip away all the layers of false pretenses, facades, sins, and varnishes of this world, and lay our souls bare before Him. He can do that only if we let Him. Only He knows what lies beneath our dark stains and sees the full potential for which He created us. "For God sees not as man sees, for man looks at the outward appearance but the Lord looks at the heart" (1 Sam. 16:7, NASB).

26

99 44/100 Percent Pure

For as long as I can remember there has been a brand of hand and body soap advertised as 99 44/100 percent pure. Mother bought and used it in our home as I was growing up. True to tradition, I too buy and use it, as do our children.

The bar of soap is white, rectangular, and uninteresting-looking with a nondescript but clean scent. Its outside wrapping is nearly the same—plain. Consumer complaints are nonexistent because it does the job that the advertisers promise. It cleans.

It isn't a harsh soap; indeed it is gentle. Its nonirritating quality is safe for a baby's skin. What more could you expect from a soap? If I would ask the manufacturer a few questions about their soap, this is what they would be. "If the soap were 100 percent pure, what else could I expect it to do? What is the missing or added .56 percent ingredient that keeps it from being 100 percent pure? Can the impurities be removed?" I'm sure I'll never know the answers to these unimportant questions, and that's OK. But, as I was thinking about this trite subject I suddenly could see the same questions applicable to a Christian's life.

God's Word has something to say about purity. Jesus said, "Blessed are the pure in heart; for they shall see God" (Matt. 5:8). David wrote, "Who shall ascend into the hill of the Lord? or who shall stand in his holy place? He that hath clean hands, and a pure heart, who hath not lifted up his soul unto vanity, nor sworn deceitfully" (Ps. 24:3-4).

Telling lies and being deceitful are not the only things which make us impure. The Bible teaches that impurity of our hands and our hearts is caused by our unwillingness to make a break with the sins of the flesh, which is our "old man," self-nature. The flesh includes our thought life. When we have been reborn the old sin nature is to be reckoned as dead. Therefore, our hands will not be busy doing evil and perverted things, nor will our hearts be on those desires. Unless we make a complete break with the world and crucify the flesh we will be like that bar of soap, only 99 44/100 percent pure.

Can one be born again and be Spirit-filled and still have an impure heart? Let's look at the life of King Saul, God's handpicked first king over Israel. First Samuel 10:6-10 says that when the Spirit of God came upon Saul he would be changed into a new man. Was he a man who served God and worshiped Him? Was he anointed by the Holy Spirit? Was he a man who from time to time walked in the flesh instead of the Spirit? Read chapter 10 verse 10. The Holy Spirit came upon Saul mightily. Chapter 11 verse 15 tells us that he sacrificed peace offerings before the Lord. Then in chapter 13 verse 8 we see him walking in the flesh of disobedience to the prophet Samuel's command stated in chapter 10 verse 8. Saul was to wait seven days in Gilgal, and Samuel said he would meet him there and make a burnt offering sacrifice with him before going into battle. Saul became a little nervous when Samuel didn't arrive at the hour he thought he should; perhaps he was an hour or two late. Saul became impatient, and his faith wavered. He decided to press on without Samuel, and offered the sacrifice alone. Of course, as soon as he had finished sacrificing, Samuel showed up. The prophet rebuked Saul for his disobedience. His disobedience was to God since God spoke through the prophets to His people.

Saul had the prerogative of walking in the Spirit with the Holy Spirit of God guiding him or walking in his own way. His choice of walking in the flesh made him unfit for ruling God's chosen people. His heart was only 99 44/100 percent pure.

It's so easy to be a Saul. It's so easy to live a life of unbelief and disobedience; but God is looking for a people who have clean hands and a pure heart. How can we have clean hands and a pure heart? Ephesians 5:22-27 sheds light on the question, and I believe gives us the answer. First, we are to have loving submission to God, then die to our self-will on the cross of self-denial. Next is the knowledge that we are cleansed, washed, purified—our sins forgiven—by the promise of the pardon of sins (1 John 1:9). By the confession of our sins, complete submission to God, and making His desire for us our desire, we will have clean hands and a pure heart. When our hearts are pure then we shall experience the promise of Jesus: "Blessed are the pure in heart; for they shall see God."

27

The Eyes of the Lord

The whirr of helicopter blades overhead droned in my ears. This time I wouldn't let that sound disturb my concentration on the cars moving before me. While driving, in times past, I would have opened my window, hung out my head, and while trying to keep my eyes focused on the road, would have waved to my husband who was flying the chopper above me. If the children were with me they too would hang their heads out of the windows, wave, and yell loudly, "Hi, Daddy." This time I would just wave.

Jim had been selected as lunar module pilot for *Apollo 15* and, since the lunar module flies similarily to a helicopter, he needed to keep current and proficient in the helicopter. The more he flew the more skilled and attuned his hands, feet, and mind became to a helicopter's peculiar characteristics. Perhaps one day his and the space commander's safety might depend on his expertise in flying this aircraft. He flew anytime and everytime he could, including weekends.

Many times while flying locally he would cruise over our house. Finding the car gone, he would set out looking for his wife and family. I would often hear that familiar sound overhead while driving. First I would hear, then sense his presence, and finally see the shadow of the aircraft. Usually I would open the car window and wave. He waved back. Other times when he flew over our house I would hear him make a pass. It gave me time to run outside, look up, and wave as he made the second pass. It was one of our little secrets of staying in touch.

Today, as I look back seventeen years, tender thoughts fill my heart and mind with sweet memories.

I like to bring those scenes into focus for myself with the Word of God. Little happenings in my life often parallel one of His principles, and His Word becomes clearer to me.

God, from His vantage point in the heavenlies, is always watching over His children. Second Chronicles 16:9 bears out this truth. "For the eyes of the Lord move to and fro throughout the earth that He may strongly support those whose heart is completely His" (NASB).

I'm so glad God's eyes are on us. Regardless of where we are or what we are doing, He sees, He knows, He cares. It not only makes us feel special, but it helps us to remember to live a life that is wholly pleasing unto Him.

28

Humility for the Proud

My husband Jim, our daughter Jan, and I were fel-lowshiping with the Cornukes around our dining room table. We had just finished a light lunch and were kicking around some light banter. Bob and Sherri are a joy to be with, and we especially appreciate Bob's quick wit, keen humor, and glib tongue.

Bob and his beautiful, raven-haired wife were both police officers. He for the Orange County, California, police department and Sherri for Santa Ana, California. Bob looks like a dark-haired, mustachioed, macho Cossack straight out of *Dr. Zhivago.* He can keep us intrigued for hours while relating experiences that the two have had. This day was no exception.

Bob had been a policeman about four years when he, along with a few others, was selected for the first motorcycle police brigade of the Costa Mesa, California, police department. The department sent these elite men through an intense, three-week course of motorcycle training. It is a very dangerous part of their work because of the speed and precision required.

The day of graduation arrived, along with the press

and photographers. With all the fuss being made, Bob's pride was established and beginning to grow. He felt like he was the hottest and best-looking motorcycle policeman in the bunch.

Shortly, all the men were issued unique new uniforms for riding on their motorcycles. The black turtleneck sweater, worn under a navy-blue Eisenhower jacket, matched his hair and mustache and looked terrific with his dark brown eyes. His matching navy-blue jodhpurs were tight from the knee down for a better high-cut boot fit. The uniform was accentuated by black leather gloves and topped off with a black-and-white helmet.

Bob donned his new uniform with great pride and finished the total look with mirrored sunglasses. Smoothing his mustache just one more time, he walked out the front door. He climbed on the brand-new Kawasaki 900, complete with added police lights, radio, and a black leather saddlebag in the back, and cranked up the engine. His heart soared as he steered the motorcycle into traffic to begin a day on the beat. He spotted a few cars with the time expired on the parking meters and stopped to write some tickets. Finishing the job, he mounted the motorcycle again and cruised by a shopping center. All the storefronts were glass and, in the morning shade, they produced a mirror-like finish. He hadn't completely seen himself in full regalia on his motorcycle, and figured now was the time, as he gazed into the mirror-like windows. *You handsome dude, you,* he thought, as he quickly studied himself. *You look terrific.*

Bob didn't see the little yellow Volkswagen slowly back out of its parking place, with a girl at the wheel. He hit his brakes a little late and smashed into her rear bumper. The cycle fell over, and he was thrown upon the back of her car. His pride was severely wounded and bleeding profusely.

A smile played across my lips as I listened and a Scripture beat out a tune in my head. "Pride goes before destruction, pride goes before destruction," it drummed.

To me the most classic statement on pride in the Bible is the one that King Nebuchadnezzar made after being humbled for seven years. He had exalted himself with pride above the knowledge of God; and he had claimed greatness for himself. His punishment was to dwell with the beasts of the field and eat what they ate for those years. Afterward, God restored him to his senses and his kingdom. This was his amazing statement; "Now I Nebuchadnezzar praise, exalt, and honor the King of heaven, for all His works are true and His ways just, and He is able to humble those who walk in pride" (Dan. 4:37, NASB).

Bob would agree.

29

At the Father's Right Hand

In most families a phenomenon usually occurs at evening mealtimes around the table. Perhaps it happens because we are creatures of habit; I'm not really sure. But, it seems that when the family gathers to be seated, they always gravitate to "their position," "their chair." Have you ever noticed that? And, woe to anyone who tries to take "their" place. If that situation is true at your house let me assure you it is also true at the Irwins'.

For the past twenty-three years our eldest son, Jim, has, with rare exception, sat to the right of his father. Anyone trying to usurp that position, knowingly or unknowingly, was in for a verbal battle.

Until recently I didn't realize the significance of this unimportant seating arrangement around our table. However, when I read in my Bible that Jesus is seated at the right hand of His Father, I wanted to know more about this position. This is what great news I found.

Acts 7:55-56 tells the story of Stephen's stoning. Just as the crowd was about to pick up stones, he had a vision. He saw the heavens open and Jesus standing at the right hand of the Father. In Romans 8:34, Paul tells us that Jesus who died and was resurrected is at the Father's right hand. He also reminds us in Ephesians 1:18-23 of Christ's exalted position and why. And the apostle wants the saints to know who they are in Jesus and what their legal inheritance is.

> These are in accordance with the working of . . . His might which He brought about in Christ, when He raised Him from the dead, and seated Him at His right hand in the heavenly places, far above all rule and authority and power and dominion and every name that is named, not only in this age, but also in the one to come. And He put all things in subjection under His feet, and gave Him as head over all things to the church, which is His body, the fulness of Him who fills all in all (vv. 19*b*-23, NASB).

In chapter 2, verses 4 through 7, we see our position of honor and why.

> But God, being rich in mercy, because of His great love with which He loved us, even when we were dead in our transgressions, made us alive together with Christ (by grace you have been saved), and raised us up with Him, and seated us with Him in the heavenly places, in Christ Jesus, in order that in the ages to come, He might show the surpassing riches of His grace in kindness toward us in Christ Jesus. (NASB).

Beloved, we are *in* Christ Jesus. Since Jesus is seated at the Father's right hand, that means we are also seated there. We are *in* Christ, seated next to the Father. The right hand is a figure for the place of honor and sovereign power. That knowledge gets me to shouting, Hallelujah!

Let's go back to chapter 1, verse 21. Since God sat Jesus *above* all rule, authority, powers, dominions, and over every name that is named, not only in that age but the age to come (our age, too), and we are seated *in* Christ in the heavenlies, we have the same authority that Jesus has.

Jesus said in Luke 10:19, "Behold, I have given you authority, . . . over all, the power of the enemy, and nothing shall injure you" (NASB). He gave us His authority. Christians, we need to get plugged into the knowledge of this power source and realize this is why we can defeat Satan and his cohorts. We don't have to let them run over us, bully us, and leave us bleeding and dying on the Jericho road. Bless God, we are *victorious overcomers,* not survivors of the battle. Your authority and position have already been established by Jesus because of His position in the Father.

Next time the enemy comes to do a number on you, use your authority in the name of Jesus; and run him off with, "Thus saith the Lord!"

30

A Baby Skunk

Nearly every summer, about halfway through the season, it must be mating time for the skunks. Since they are nocturnal creatures they come alive at night. I don't know what makes them turn loose with a very undesirable, nasty odor almost nightly, unless they are marking off their territory. Whatever the reason, it makes sleeping at night very difficult for me.

One night last summer God gave me a special experience. It was nearly 11 PM, and Jim was already fast asleep. I had just slipped into my nightgown when that awful choking, asphyxiating, familiar odor reached my nostrils. *Oh no,* I thought, *how long will it take to dissipate?* Walking over to the outdoor light switch, I flipped it on, hoping to see the culprit. The big one was nowhere in sight, but my eyes were drawn to movement in the darkness. There was a baby skunk who was very busy. It was obviously practicing in earnest what its mother had told it to do. It would take four tiny steps forward, then two backward, and turn. Four steps forward, two backward, then turn, I was mesmerized.

I remembered from my youth a girl friend who had

a pet skunk named "Stinky Poo," and it used to do the same little dance. Here I was watching skunk tactics of war being practiced by a little fellow. I must have watched five minutes when a big tabby cat approached. *Oh oh, here comes trouble.* In my mind I could already anticipate what I thought would happen. Wrong. The cat had enough sense to sit closely by and watch, too. Four steps forward, two backward, then turn. Another ten minutes passed before the cat tired of the show and sauntered off into the night. Not me, I was sure I'd miss something if I went to bed.

Presently, another night visitor appeared. This time a large skunk waddled down the hill close to where the little one was practicing. *For sure, this time,* I thought, *we are going to have trouble.* On the contrary, big daddy just kept ambling. I was so impressed with the baby skunk's determination to hang in there with its practicing and not be deterred by anything, even a bright light beaming down on its territory.

By this time nearly a half hour had passed. I switched off the light and headed for bed. Somehow sleep wouldn't come. I couldn't get that amazing experience out of my mind. "Surely, Lord, You have just taught me an important lesson, but what?"

As I lay awake, God quickened to my heart a verse from the Book of Luke (9:61). Here our Lord is dealing with halfhearted disciples. Some of us say "Yes" to Jesus too because we want all the benefits He has to offer us without any commitment to Him. That's why Jesus' reply in verse 62 was so tart. "No one, after putting his hand to the plow and looking back, is fit for the kingdom of God" (NASB).

"The image which our Lord used was, as usual, one that went home to the personal experience of His hearers. They were of a peasant class, and they knew that the eye of the ploughman, if he is to do his work well, must look straight before him at the line of the furrow which he is making. To look back, while working, is to mar the work entirely. The man who so looks is therefore disqualified for the work of God's kingdom."[1]

I believe Jesus is saying to us, "Once you have made a commitment to Me, go forward and let nothing or anyone deter that commitment. Follow Me at all costs and don't become distracted with anything of this world." Like the little skunk, who was not moved by anything that came his way, so are we to be in following Jesus.

I'm so glad He allowed me to watch that busy little fellow that night. I certainly learned another lesson He wanted to teach me, a lesson on commitment.

1. *Ellicott's Commentary on the Whole Bible* (Grand Rapids, MI: Zondervan Publishing Co., 1959), Vol. iii., p. 290.

31
Joey

Crash! Crackle! Another bolt and flash of lightning tore through the silent evening's airspace as I stood on the back porch watching the eastern sky. Then the resounding thunder pierced my eardrums, and a shudder went through my body.

Observing a summer thunder and lightning storm in Colorado Springs had kept me totally unaware of my surroundings until I felt a frantic tug at my skirt. My newly adopted Vietnamese son was jabbering wildly in his native tongue and trying, with all his three-year-old might, to pull me indoors. Fear blazed from his big brown eyes, and terror was written all over his little brown face. Scooping him up in my arms, I tried to comfort his frightened heart by telling him it wasn't the enemy bombing our home but, in fact, was a beautiful display, in the heavens, from God. He didn't understand a word I spoke, but my lack of fear seemed to quiet his spirit, and he snuggled close to my breast.

The Bible says that fear has torment or punishment (see 1 John 4:18). We were to see that punishment manifested in our Joey many, many times over the next few years as he awakened in the middle of the night, screaming with fearful nightmares from his wartorn past. Fear seemed to rule over his sleep and often overtook his daytime activities, too.

Romans 6:16 says, "Don't you realize that you can choose your own master?" (TLB). The one to whom you offer yourself will take you and be your master and you his slave. Unknowingly, Joey had become a slave of fear. It ruled his life. He was too young to understand the meaning, but he lived the consequences.

As I read 1 John 4:18-19 once again, I tried to understand what the apostle John was telling Christians concerning fear and how perfect love would cast out that evil spirit of fear. It didn't make sense to me exactly how love could be the answer to fear. I thought that faith was the opposite of fear and a lack of faith the reason for fearing. As I sought the Lord for understanding, His words to me were, "Faith and love work together. You don't have faith in someone you don't love, and you don't love someone you don't have faith in."

Ellicott's Commentary explains it this way. "When love is perfect, fear dwindles to nothing, is absolutely expelled. Love, seeking to be perfect, and finding fear alongside of it, will diligently seek out the cause of fear, perfect itself by getting rid of the cause, and so get rid of the fear."[1]

As our love in and for Christ becomes more stable, it does replace our fears with faith. Christ then becomes our Master, and we are the slaves of His perfect will for us. We become His slaves because of our love for Him; and in that love there is no room for fear or its consequences of punishment and torment.

When Joey believed in and trusted our love for him, his war memories and fears were laid to rest and became the past. The Scripture really is true. "There is no fear in love, but perfect love casts out fear" (1 John 4:18, NASB).

> Fear knocked at the door,
> Faith answered it
> And no one was there.

---

1. *Ellicott's Commentary on the Whole Bible* (Grand Rapids, MI: Zondervan Publishing Co., 1959), Vol. iv, p. 489

32

Untempered and Broken

Shortly after the flight of *Apollo 15* in 1971, the crew and their wives were invited to New York City for a ticker-tape parade. Mayor John Lindsay and his wife were gracious to us and gave each crew member a beautiful gift of very costly Steuben glassware.

For years, it graced our home on a special shelf. It was taken down only for washing or a special occasion for serving a dessert. Each time it was used, I remembered the directions for washing. The label said, "Wash in warm soapy water; do not use hot water." It didn't say why. Carefully, I would wash the dish and put it away on its shelf, once again awaiting a special day or a cleaning day.

One cleaning day, I became especially hurried so I didn't take my usual careful time with the glassware on the shelf. The sink was full of warm soapy water and each item had a good dunking. Rinsing each with care, I finally came to the Steuben treasure and quickly decided just this once to use a hotter rinse water so it would have an extra sparkle. I didn't have the dish under the hot water spigot for more than five seconds, but it was five seconds too long. Instantly, I was holding two pieces instead of one. I gasped, looked down at my hands, and my heart just sank.

You see, the glass hadn't been tempered by a high degree of heat, then stressed by cold to give it strength. It was more for looks, or perhaps for a candy dish.

I've thought about that dish many times since as it relates so well to tempered and untempered people. The tempered Christian is more like a beautiful piece of Waterford crystal. It is tempered for much use in the home and does not sit idly on a shelf as an object of art.

Paul says in Romans 5:1-4, that even though we are happy knowing our hope of glory in God, we are also to be happy in our tribulations. Why? Because "tribulations bring about perseverence; and perseverence, proven character; and proven character, hope" (NASB).

The dictionary definitions of "tribulation" are: Affliction, hardship, distress, adversity, and suffering. To temper glass means to produce internal stress by sudden cooling from a low red heat. Have you ever felt the low red heat of a hardship? The working through of our hardships produces a tempered character. The tempering of our character comes from many tribulations. Luke states, in Acts 14:22, "Through many tribulations we must enter the kingdom of God" (NASB). As our character is being proven by the process of many trials it gives way to hope, and Jesus is our only hope of glory.

The tempering process makes our character more like that of our Savior and makes us fit for His kingdom. Our character is all we will take with us to heaven, therefore it must be tempered and proven.

We are to be like the beautiful cut glass Waterford crystal, qualified and transparent. We need to be used daily without concern of hot water breaking us and rendering us useless. In fact, the more we are used by God, the more we are depended upon, and the more we are appreciated and trusted by others.

I'd rather be a piece of Waterford crystal for Jesus any day than a Steuben art object that is placed into hot water only once and then cracks and breaks. Wouldn't you?

33

A Handful of Ribbons

Dear Sister Ford wore funny blue-tinted, wire-rimmed glasses, and her hair was tied up in a small tight bun on the back of her head. She had a petite build and was very bony. How well I remember her from my childhood! I saw her only once a week, at church. It was as though she had an assigned seat in an assigned row. She was always there, taking part in the service. As a child, I don't know whether she amused me or intrigued me more or maybe it was the other way around. Perhaps both.

I knew Mrs. Ford was a widow, or so I had heard, since she was always sitting alone. What really fascinated me was watching the expressions on her happy face as the pastor preached his sermon. I don't remember the sermons; I couldn't watch her and listen to the preacher, too. Her reactions were sometimes awe, with her mouth forming an O, or a big smile, while nodding her head in agreement, often even an amen. Her facial expressions were like watching a pantomime.

I remember the day I met this fascinating lady at her

front door. The church had an annual drive to gather money for the poor, and I was with my friends soliciting from door to door. We rang the doorbell and gave her our pitch. She said, "Just a moment," and went to fetch her purse. After dropping some coins into our tin cans she made this unusual statement. "I haven't missed Sunday School in thirty-five years. I have ribbons for every quarter of perfect attendance, and when I die I don't want any flowers on my casket; I only want all my ribbons placed there for a testimony." Not knowing what else to say, we thanked her for her contribution, then turned and walked away. I tucked her words down deep in my heart. I didn't know what else to do with them. They distinctly made an indelible impression on me.

As I look back on that experience, everything comes into perspective. There are saints in the church who love Jesus very much and never miss attending and, yet, what is their testimony? Ribbons on a casket? It grieves me just to think about it.

Jesus said, "Truly, truly, I say to you, he who believes in Me, the works that I do shall he do also; and greater works than these shall he do; because I go to the Father. And whatever you ask in My name, that will I do, that the Father may be glorified in the Son" (John 14:12-13, NASB). We who believe in Jesus as the Son of God are to do the same works Jesus did. What works did Jesus do? He preached His Father's words, taught, healed the sick, cast out demons, and raised the dead. Where does that leave most of us Christians? Our testimony should be the works of

Jesus, done with the same Holy Ghost power. "And [even] greater works," He said.

Are we doing the works Jesus did, and are signs (miracles) following us, our ministry, to confirm the Word of God? Are we asking Jesus, in His name, to do the miracles so His Father will receive the glory? This is a heavy question, beloved, but I believe God would have us search our hearts to find the answer. Maybe it's time to be quiet before the Lord and examine, with a fine-tooth comb, our testimony and what it is saying to a lost and dying world.

"So then, when the Lord Jesus had spoken to them, He was received up into heaven, and sat down at the right hand of God. And they [the disciples] went out and preached everywhere, while the Lord worked with them, and confirmed the word by the signs that followed" (Mark 16:19-20, NASB).

We need to be about our Father's business just as Jesus was about His Father's business, and the Father will confirm His Word with signs following. God is looking for willing and obedient servants. He is looking for servants who will believe Him and trust Him to make signs follow the preaching and teaching of His Word. Will you go and do the works that Jesus did so His Father will be glorified, or will a drawerful of ribbons be your testimony?

34

Rescue the Perishing

Jim, Jan, and I were checked into our favorite gourmet restaurant-chalet in all the world. It is nestled among the fragrant orange groves of a small town in Southern Florida. One of the unique qualities about Chalet Suzanne is that it has a grass landing strip for small airplanes next to the restaurant, which overlooks a small lake. Many private plane owners fly in for a sumptuous lunch or dinner, and often spend the night.

We were dressed for dinner, but I was still lying flat on my back on the bed, trying to ease the pain of an injury I had sustained two days earlier while playing tennis. All of a sudden, I heard a four-seater, propeller-driven engine on the landing strip; I didn't know whether they were taking off or landing. Just as abruptly as I had heard the engine, now I didn't hear it. My mind told me something was wrong. Airplane engines don't just suddenly stop; it takes a little while for them to wind down.

I called to Jim to have a look and see what the problem was. He walked out on the porch and couldn't believe his eyes. Much to his astonishment, a

plane had just landed in the lake. The pilot had over-
shot the runway. All I could imagine was dead people
and a wrecked aircraft. Jim hurriedly ran down the
stairs to alert the front desk to the calamity. Within
seconds the attendant at the switchboard was clanging
the fire-warning bell. The owners, Carl and Vita Hin-
shaw, came racing to the scene.

Immediately our daughter, Jan, and her Air Force
officer friend, Mark, stripped off their blue jeans and
shirts, ran to the edge of the lake, and dived in. Every
stroke counted. Time was not on their side; the aircraft
was beginning to sink. Mark outswam Jan, by seconds,
and reached the pilot's door. He was already trying to
get out, but the passenger, his wife, had been knocked
unconscious. As Mark was helping the pilot get his
wife out, a rescue fire truck and an ambulance came
screaming by.

The restaurant had emptied, and others were joining us near the outdoor pool as we watched the rescue
mission. Jan had retreated from the lake and stood
shivering beside us. She said they had all the help they
needed, and she didn't want to hamper the operations.
We watched as Mark and the pilot lifted his unconscious wife on to a flotation device and swam with her
to the shore. Moments later the ambulance left for the
hospital with its precious cargo. All the spectators de-
parted, except the five of us. We stayed ten minutes
longer and watched as the little plane sank to the bottom. The only visible object in the fast-approaching
darkness was the glow of the aircraft's red and white
navigational lights from the bottom of the lake.

Nearly a year later the pilot and his wife wanted to do something extra special for Mark. They found out he was an Air Force officer and recommended him for a bravery award. It was their way of saying, "Many grateful thanks for saving my life."

As I think about their gracious thanks for being rescued, I am reminded of another kind of rescue. The rescue by God of His children. The psalmist wrote, "Save me, O my God. The floods have risen. Deeper and deeper I sink in the mire; the waters rise around me" (Ps. 69:1, TLB). "Then they cried to the Lord in their troubles, and he rescued them! He led them from the darkness and shadow of death and snapped their chains. Oh, that these men would praise the Lord for his lovingkindness and for all his wonderful deeds!" (Ps. 107:13-15, TLB)

When we need help and rescuing from problems that we have no control over, Jesus is always there. He will truly lift us out of the miry pits of darkness and put His saving arms of love around us. We need to praise and thank Him for His constant loving-kindness. He is merciful to His children.

35

Running the Race

The month was April, the year 1955. Our track meet was over for another year at Walla Walla College Academy, and I was on my way home. In my possession were five colored ribbons, one blue, two red, and two white.

I never thought it was possible to take a blue ribbon from Sherry; she was the fastest runner in school. I was always second place to her, when it came to foot races. With no encouragement from anyone I was still a determined runner. The only reason I was five seconds faster in this event was my nimble fingers. You see, this event wasn't a track event. It was field day at the school, and this race was to tie a necktie properly on a person at the other end of the field, then run back to the starting line. The rest of the prizes were for legally marked-off distances. I always tried my very best to beat Sherry, but there is always only one winner. Sometimes I wonder if my motives had been pure, would I have been the winner more often? My jealousy in Sherry's speed was my motive.

The apostle Paul, in his Letter to the Hebrews, gives

a word of exhortation to them, as well as us, concerning running a race. In this instance he is talking about faith; however, he uses this verbiage of the Olympic-type games from Greece to make a spiritual point. It still applies to all spiritual races, as well as other races. In chapter 12 verse 1 he advises us to lay aside, or put away, every sin which habitually hampers our running and run the race with endurance. I was beset with the sin of jealousy. It encumbered my race so much that it was difficult to concentrate on running well. Instead of keeping my eyes only on the goal, I'd sometimes glance over my shoulder to see how close Sherry was to me. It was, at those times, that she would pass me and win.

In 1 Corinthians 9:24-27 Paul puts it all together.

> In a race, everyone runs but only one person gets first prize. So run your race to win. To win the contest you must deny yourselves many things that would keep you from doing your best. An athlete goes to all this trouble just to win a blue ribbon or a silver cup, but we do it for a heavenly reward that never disappears. So I run straight to the goal with purpose in every step. I fight to win. I'm not just shadowboxing or playing around. Like an athlete I punish my body, treating it roughly, training it to do what it should, not what it wants to do. Otherwise I fear that after enlisting others for the race, I myself might be declared unfit and ordered to stand aside (TLB).

Putting aside our willful sinning, we will be declared fit for the race and win our eternal heavenly reward. The heavenly crown of righteous glory is worth it all, dear one. Run your race to win.

36

The Living Cross

It was a lovely Sunday morning in France. Jim would be speaking at the eleven o'clock service. In about thirty minutes the worshipers would begin to assemble in the church.

We walked through the narrow doorway into the small sanctuary. It seated about one hundred and fifty. My eyes were immediately riveted to the front wall. I stood motionless, unwilling to move, and gasped in awe. There it hung before us—the living cross. I could not speak. The Holy Spirit was doing the talking deep within my spirit. A new awareness of the cross, a new awareness of its meaning, flooded my soul. The experience was so moving I wasn't sure I could share it. But I must, lest the message burst within me.

The cross was ordinary looking with a few knotholes scattered across its form. It had been sanded and finished with a glossy sheen. I have seen many elegant-looking crosses that spoke nothing to my heart. They were almost meaningless to the observer. But this one, ah, it was different.

On the floor, about four feet from the base of the

cross, sat a small square planter. In the planter grew a
lush green vine sustained by the sunshine from a large
window adjacent to the front wall. The vine grew
upward toward the sunshine until it touched the horizontal structure of the cross. With the help from a
loving hand, it gracefully began to wind around the
cross. Up, down, and around it grew, leaning gently
upon the cross, until, at the end, its leafy face turned
heavenward.

All through the sermon, my attention was drawn to
the cross. I must etch it in my mind, but that was not
enough. As I listened to Jim speak, I sketched that
beautiful vine entwined on the cross. I wanted to remember it forever.

It seems to me that in most cases the cross has almost
become meaningless. It has become sterile instead of
fertile. It has become a neckpiece instead of a heart-
piece. It has become a gaudy, cold showpiece instead
of the heat of shame. We have violated the humility of
the cross.

Looking at the one facing me, God once again drove
into my heart the nails of the meaning of the cross. The
cross means death. Christ died in my place, for my sins,
on that cross. Sin always requires blood for atonement.
Sin separates us from God and needs *at-one-ment*. At
one with God means a giving up of my life-style and
taking up the cross, His life-style. The cross is a life-
style of self-denial. It means dying to my will and
making God's will for me my will.

"Today, if anyone preaches self-denial as a condition
of discipleship, you can hear the comments afterwards:

'old fashioned,' 'harsh,' 'legalistic.' I dare say that our Lord would have as much trouble finding acceptance among our preachers today as He did among the religious leaders of His day" (Keith Green, *The Missing Parts*).

A. W. Tozer says this about the cross. "The cross is the most revolutionary thing ever to appear among men. The cross of Roman times knew no compromise; it never made concessions. It won all its arguments by killing its opponents and silencing them for good. It spared not Christ but slew Him the same as the rest. He was alive when they hung Him on that cross and completely dead when they took Him off of it. That was the cross the first time it appeared in Christian history.

"With perfect knowledge of all this, Christ said, 'If any man will come after me, let him deny himself, take up his cross and follow Me.' So the cross not only brought Christ's life to an end, it also ends the first life, the old life of everyone of His true followers . . . this and nothing less is true Christianity. We must do something about the cross, and there's only one of two things we can do—FLEE IT OR DIE UPON IT!"

Well, friends, that's still the story, the meaning, and the decision of the cross today. What will you do with the cross? What will you do with Jesus? Will you flee it and spend eternity separated from God, or will you die upon it, to be resurrected and live in and with Jesus for eternity?

God still gives you the choice.

Dear Reader,

If you have chosen to follow Jesus today for the first time, please write to me and let me know.

May God richly bless your life as you follow the way of the cross.

Victoriously yours,

Mary Irwin
P. O. Box 1387
Colorado Springs,
Colorado 80906